EVERLASTING FLORAL GIFTS

EVERLASTING FLORAL GIFTS

by Rob Pulleyn
and
Claudette Mautor

A Sterling/**Lark** book

Sterling Publishing Co., Inc., New York

Published in paperback 1991 by Sterling Publishing Company, Inc.
387 Park Avenue South, New York, N.Y. 10016

© 1990 by Altamont Press

A Sterling/Lark Book

Produced by Altamont Press, Inc.
50 College Street, Asheville, NC 28801
Design and Production: Judy Clark
Typesetting: Elaine Thompson
Photography: Evan A. Bracken

To my constant garden companions: frogs, snails, and critters—CM

Library of Congress Cataloging-in-Publication Data
Pulleyn, Rob
        Everlasting floral gifts/Rob Pulleyn and Claudette Mautor.
                p.   cm.
        "A Sterling/Lark Book."
        ISBN 0-8069-5826-X
        1. Flower arrangement.   2. Wreaths.   3. Potpourris (Scented
floral mixtures)   4. Flower language.   5. Nature craft.   6. Gifts.
I. Mautor, Claudette.   II. Title
SB449.P85   1989
745.92--dc20   89-21909
                                                          CIP

Distributed in Canada by Sterling Publishing
℅ Canadian Manda Group, P.O. Box 920, Station U
Toronto, Ontario, Canada M8Z 5P9
Distributed in Great Britain and Europe by Cassell PLC
Villiers House, 41/47 Strand, London WC2N 5JE, England
Distributed in Australia by Capricorn Ltd.
P.O. Box 665, Lane Cove, NSW 2066

Printed in Hong Kong
All rights reserved

Sterling ISBN 0-8069-5826-X Trade
                0-8069-5827-8 Paper

Contents

Introduction

While the introduction may be the first page you usually read in a book, it's traditionally the last page the author writes.

We started this book with only a short outline of the subjects we wanted to cover. We had a list of experienced designers who we'd worked with on *The Wreath Book*, our intrepid photographer, and a fascination with the unique everlasting floral gifts Claudette was creating with flowers rich in historical meaning.

"To me," Claudette says, "the marvel of flower language is like the marvel of music—you don't need to be an expert musician to be enveloped by music's moods, melodies, and messages. Like music, flowers speak to the very soul. One need only look and listen."

As Claudette's research of flowers with historical meaning neared completion, everyone connected with the book began to appreciate how simple it is to convey personal sentiments and wishes with floral gifts . . . and how difficult it is to convey these same thoughts with words.

Dried flowers and herbs (referred to generically as "everlastings" in this book) allow us to enjoy the glorious beauty of nature's gardens year 'round. They can be used in such a variety of ways—potpourris, wreaths, garlands, topiaries, sachets, pomanders, and arrangements, to name just a few—that boredom is never a possibility. Although there are over 100 projects in this book, the most important projects—yours—are not included, and we hope you'll approach this book with confidence in your own innate creativity.

We've noticed that many beginners get discouraged halfway through a project, convinced that it looks awful and will never turn out "right." To that we have three responses: feeling discouraged is normal; don't worry about it; and keep going. How many of your favorite recipes look appealing halfway through the cooking process?

Most books are linear. They go from chapter to chapter with some logical order. We guess there's some logic here, but not much. After the opening sections on the basics of drying and preparing everlastings, each chapter exists independently. Feel free to wander through the chapters in any order you like. Even consider mixing ideas from different chapters: glue a potpourri recipe to a wreath base, for instance, or create a topiary with the everlastings from a favorite arrangement.

The only real secret to working with everlastings is to relax and have fun. So sit back, relax, and spend a few hours discovering the incredible joys of creating special gifts with everlastings.

—*Rob Pulleyn and Claudette Mautor*

Everlasting Floral Gifts

All flowers are beautiful, delighting our senses of sight and smell. They renew our appreciation for the delicate beauty of life, and make special occasions even more special. In addition to their beauty, many flowers also radiate a message, a unique meaning that often speaks more directly than words. And while almost everyone is familiar with the meanings of different colors of roses (red for true love, white for purity, yellow for jealousy or passionate love), the special meanings of many other varieties of flowers are virtually unknown.

The sources of flower meanings are entwined deep in the roots of human history, folklore, and mythology. And while it's often difficult to pinpoint the exact derivation of a particular flower's meaning, these meanings were in no way arbitrarily assigned. Connecting meanings with flowering plants can be traced back historically as early as the Middle Ages, when flowers and herbs were grown for culinary and medicinal reasons. Arthurian legends, for example, hold that Merlin the Magician and his fellow enchanters used rosemary to cast spells that would create prosperity for their clients. At the time, rosemary was used as a seasoning in stews, and since starvation was so rampant, the few people who had enough food to worry about seasonings were considered prosperous. Two other meanings commonly associated with rosemary—health and wisdom—can also be attributed to social conditions in the Middle Ages, since the few who had plentiful food were able to nourish their bodies and minds.

In the early 1500s, when stable food and housing became more the norm, people began growing flowers simply for their beauty. Ocean voyages and exploration became more frequent, and travelers brought back many new species of flowers. Meanings for these flowers often were derived from special characteristics of the flower's homeland or from personality quirks of the royalty that ruled a flower's former soil. Other flower meanings evolved when the flower's original name was translated into the language of its new home. The word "juniper," for example, comes from the Latin, meaning youth-producing; thus the coniferous tree juniper has come to mean perpetual vitality. Similarly, the foreign name for the amaranth flower translated to never-waxing-old, and became a symbol for immortality.

In mythological stories there are several explanations for flower meanings. One day the young huntress of Greek mythology, Daphne, was enjoying her freedom in the woods, when Apollo, the god of light, saw her and proclaimed his love. Racing through the woods to escape him, Daphne called out to her father, the river god Peneus, for help. Just as Apollo was about to catch her, she came to her father's river and cried out again. Suddenly Daphne felt her body numbing, her feet anchoring to the ground, and leaves sprouting from her arms. To keep his daughter from harm, Daphne's father had turned her into a laurel tree. Apollo watched her metamorphosis with great sadness, crying ". . . at least you shall be my tree; with your leaves my victors shall wreathe their bows. . ." Laurel was later recorded in history as a decoration for merit and glory, and the Romans used it to decorate their olympic champions.

Flowers have also developed meanings through religious and artistic uses. Christmas trees and Easter lilies are two examples. Early painters would often place a flower in the hand of a model to emit a special meaning.

Gifts made from symbolic everlasting flowers are more than one-dimensional. While their beauty is appealing to our senses, the meanings they emit become treasured sentiments in our hearts. And because they're made with everlastings, they can be displayed in the homes of loved ones for years to come. The charts on the following pages can be used to select flowers with meanings specially suited to an occasion. Mix and match several meanings together to form beautiful floral messages — and beautiful gifts.

Anniversaries bring sentiments portrayed by the flowers. Dogwood for lasting relationships, muted evergreens for perpetual vitality and color, which says we are integral and we protect one another.

Plants and Meanings

Common	Latin	Meaning
Abutilon	*Abutilon*	The future is full of promise
Ageratum	*Ageratum*	Indispensable for progress
Aloe	*Aloe*	The healing herb
Amaranth (globe)	*Amaranthus*	Unchangeable
Amaryllis	*Amaryllis*	Pride
Angelica	*Angelica*	Inspiration
Aster (white/yellow)	*Aster*	The beginning of all progress
Auricula	*Primula auricula*	Painting
Azalea, Indian	*Rhododendron*	True to the end
Bachelor's Button	*Centaurea cyanus*	Single blessedness
Balsam	*Impatiens*	Impatience
Basil, sweet	*Ocimum basilicum*	It fills the heart with joy
Bay, sweet	*Laurus nobilis*	Reward of merit
Bee balm	*Monarda*	The enchantress
Begonia	*Begonia*	Ethereal love
Betony	*Stachys*	Surprise
Birch	*Betula*	Meekness
Bittersweet	*Celastrus*	Truth
Broom	*Cytisus, Genista*	Neatness, humility
Butterfly Bush	*Buddleia*	Refinement
Butterfly Weed (orange)	*Asclepias tuberosa*	The physical mind eager to understand and be transformed
(yellow)		An important step toward realization
Cabbage	*Brassica*	Profit
Cactus		Warmth
Calendula	*Calendula officinalis*	The decision to go to the very end
Candytuft	*Iberis*	Indifference; peace and calm
Canterbury Bells	*Campanula medium*	Acknowledgement
Cardamon	*Elettaria cardamomum*	Knowing exactly what to say, with neither too many, nor too few words
Carnation, red	*Dianthus*	Alas for my poor heart
Celosia, plume red	*Amaranthaceae*	Intense aspirations but ignorant of the means
Celosia, plume yellow		Has much to say and says it fully
Celosia, round yellow		Let your mind be capable of foreseeing the perfections of tomorrow
Chamomile	*Anthemis*	Energy in adversity
Cherry Tree	*Prunus*	Good education
Chickweed	*Stellaria media*	Rendezvous
Chicory	*Chichorium intybus*	Removing obstacles; promotes frugality
Chives	*Allium*	Protection, healing
Chrysanthemum	*Chrysanthemum*	Truth
Cineraria	*Senecio*	Everbright
Clematis	*Clematis*	Mental beauty
Clover, red	*Trifolium pratense*	Industry
Cloves	*Caryophyllus aromaticus*	Dignity
Conifers		Perpetual vitality; a vitality that is not affected by external influences
Coreopsis	*Compositae*	Always cheerful
Corn	*Zea mays*	Riches

Part Used	Category
Blossom	Trees/shrubs
Blossom	Flowers
Leaves	Herbs
Blossom	Flowers
Blossom	Flowers
Blossom, leaves	Herbs
Blossom	Flowers
Blossom	Flowers
Blossom	Trees/shrubs
Blossom	Flowers
Blossom	Flowers
Blossom, branch/stem, leaves	Herbs, vegetables, fruit, spice, seasoning, flavoring
Leaves	Trees/shrubs
Blossom, Leaves	Flowers, herbs
Blossom	Flowers
Blossom	Flowers
Blossom, branch/stem, leaves	Trees/shrubs
Leaves	Spice, seasoning, flavoring
Blossom, branch/stem, leaves	Flowers
Blossom	Trees/Shrubs
Blossom	Flowers
Blossom, leaves	Vegetables, fruit
Blossom, branch/stem	Flowers
Blossom	Flowers
Blossom, leaves	Flowers
Blossom	Flowers
Leaves	Herbs
Blossom	Flowers
Blossom	Flowers
Blossom	Flowers
Blossom	Flowers
Blossom, branch/stem, leaves	Flowers, herbs
Blossom, branch/stem, leaves	Trees/shrubs
Blossom, branch/stem, leaves	Herbs
Blossom, root	Flowers, herbs
Blossom, leaves, root fruit	Flowers, herbs, vegetables
Blossom	Flowers
Blossom	Flowers
Blossom	Spice, seasoning, flavoring
Blossom, leaves	Flowers
Seed/fruit	Vines
Branch/stem	Trees/shrubs
Blossom	Flowers
Leaves, seed/fruit	Vegetables, fruit

Common	Latin	Meaning
Corn Cockle	*Agrostemma githago*	Duration
Cranberry	*Vaccinium*	Hardness
Daffodil	*Narcissus*	Chivalry, regard
Dahlia, single	*Dahlia*	Good taste
Daisy, garden	*Chrysanthemum*	I share your sentiment
Daisy, ox eye	*C. Leucanthemum*	A token
Dandelion	*Taraxacum*	Oracle
Dill	*Anethum graveolens*	Protection
Dock	*Rumex*	Patience
Dogwood	*Cornus florida*	Durability
Echinacea	*Echinacea angustifolia*	Strength
Elderberry	*Sambucus canadensis*	Charm envelopes and conquers by an inexhaustible sweetness
Elm	*Ulmus*	Dignity
Eucalyptus	*Eucalyptus*	Protection
Evening Primrose	*Oenothera biennis*	Inconstancy
Evergreen		Poverty
Fern		Sincerity
Fuchsia, scarlet	*Fuchsia*	Taste
Garlic	*Allium sativum*	Protection
Geranium	*Pelargonium*	Spiritual happiness; calm and smiling; nothing can disturb
Germander	*Teucrium*	Health
Gladiolus	*Gladiolus*	Strength of character
Goldenrod	*Solidago*	Mental sincerity; essential for integral honesty
Gooseberry	*Ribes*	Anticipation
Gourds	*Cucurbita*	Bulk
Grape, wild	*Vitis*	Charity
Grass		Utility, submission
Hawthorne	*Crataegus*	Hope
Heath	*Erica*	Solitude
Hemp	*Eupatorium cannabinum*	Fate
Holly	*Ilex*	Foresight
Hollyhock	*Alcea*	Prolific, fruitful
Honeysuckle	*Lonicera fragrantissima*	Bonds of love; sweet disposition
Houseleek	*Sempervivum*	Domestic economy
Hyacinth	*Hyacinthus*	Sport, game, play
Iris	*Iris*	Message
Ivy	*Hedera*	Assiduous to please; lasting attachment, modest
Lady's Mantle	*Alchemilla*	Love
Larkspur	*Delphinium*	Health, lightness
Larkspur, pink	*Delphinium*	Fickleness
Laurel	*Laurus*	Glory
Lavender	*Lavandula*	Distrust, love, sleep, chastity
Leaves		Sadness
Lemon Grass	*Cymbopogon citratus*	You bring help to him who knows how to use it

Part Used	Category
Blossom	Flowers
Leaves, seed/fruit	Vegetables, fruit
Blossom	Flowers
Blossom	Flowers
Blossom	Flowers
Blossom	Flowers
Blossom, leaves, root	Flowers, herbs, vegetables, fruit
Blossom, leaves, seed/fruit	Flowers, herbs, spice, seasoning, flavoring
Blossom	Flowers, herbs
Blossom	Trees/shrubs
Blossom	Flowers, herbs
Blossom/seed/fruit	Herbs/trees/shrubs
Blossom, branch/stem, leaves	Vegetables, fruit
Branch/stem, leaves	Trees/shrubs
Blossom	Flowers
Branch/stem, seed/fruit	Trees/shrubs
Leaves	Flowers
Blossom	Flowers
Blossom, leaves, root	Flowers, herbs, vegetables, fruit, spice, seasoning, flavoring
Blossom/leaves	Flowers/herbs
Blossom, leaves	Flowers, herbs
Blossom	Flowers
Blossom	Flowers, herbs
Branch/stem, leaves, root	Trees/shrubs, vegetables, fruit
Blossom, seed/fruit	Flowers, vegetables, fruit, vines
Branch/stem, seed/fruit	Vegetables, fruit, vines
Blossom, branch/stem, leaves	Flowers
Blossom, branch/stem	Trees/shrubs
Blossom, branch/stem, leaves	Flowers
Blossom/leaves	Herbs
Branch/stem, leaves, seed/fruit	Trees/shrubs
Blossom	Flowers
Blossom, branch/stem, leaves	Spice, seasoning, flavoring
Blossom, leaves, root	Flowers, herbs, vegetables, fruit, spice, seasoning, flavoring
Blossom	Flowers
Blossom	Flowers
Branch/stem, leaves	Spice, seasoning, flavoring
Blossom, leaves	Flowers
Blossom	Flowers
Blossom	Flowers
Branch/stem, leaves	Trees/shrubs
Blossom, leaves	Herbs, spice, seasoning, flavoring
Leaves	Trees/shrubs
Blossom/branch/stem/leaves/seed/fruit	Flowers

Common	Latin	Meaning
Lilac, purple	*Syringa*	First emotions of love
Lilac, white	*Syringa*	Youthful innocence
Lily, day	*Lilium*	Coquetry
Lotus	*Nelumbo*	Eloquence
Lupin	*Lupinus polyphylus*	One goes through many stages but one will arrive
Magnolia	*Magnolia*	Dignity
Maple	*Acer rubrum*	A flame that illuminates but never burns
Marigold	*Tagetus*	Grief, dispair
Marjoram	*Origanum*	Blushes
Mint	*Mentha*	Virtue
Mistletoe	*Phoradendron flavescens*	I surmount difficulties
Moss		Maternal love
Mushroom		Suspicion
Oats	*Avena*	The soul of music
Palm		Victory
Pansy	*Viola*	Thoughts
Parsley	*Petroselinum crispum*	Festivity
Peach	*Prunus persica*	Love, longevity, wishes
Petunia	*Petunia*	Never dispair
Potato	*Solanum tuberosum*	Benevolence
Potentilla	*Potentilla*	Protection
Primrose	*Primula*	Sadness
Pussy Willow	*Salix discolor*	The future a promise yet unrealized
Queen Anne's Lace	*Dausus carota*	Purity in the blood can not be obtained except by the absence of desire
Rose	*Rosa*	Love
Rose, Carolina		Love is dangerous
Rose, single		Simplicity
Rosebud, red		Pure and lovely
Rosemary	*Rosmarinus*	Remembrance
Sage	*Salvia*	Domestic virtue, wisdom, ageless
Stock	*Matthiola*	Promptness, lasting beauty
Sunflower, tall	*Helianthus*	Haughtiness
Sweet Pea	*Lathyrus odoratus*	Gentleness; always gracious and wishing to give pleasure
Thistle	*Cirsium*	Austerity
Thyme	*Thymus*	Activity
Tulip, red	*Tulipa*	Declaration of love
Tulip, yellow		Hopeless love
Violet, blue		Faithfulness
Violet, yellow		Rural happiness
Violet, sweet	*Viola odorata*	Modesty
Windflower	*Anemone*	Fragile elegance
Wisteria	*Wistaria*	Rare and charming is your presence
Xeranthemum	*Xeranthemum*	Cheerfulness under adversity
Zinnia	*Zinnia*	Thoughts of absent friends

Part Used	Category
Blossom	Trees/shrubs
Blossom	Trees/shrubs
Blossom	Flowers
Blossom	Flowers
Blossom	Flowers
Blossom, leaves	Trees/shrubs
Leaves	Trees/shrubs
Blossom	Flowers, herbs
Blossom, leaves	Herbs, spice, seasoning, flavoring
Blossom, leaves	Herbs, spice, seasoning, flavoring
Branch/stem, leaves, seed/fruit	Flowers
Blossom, branch/stem, leaves, seed/fruit	Flowers
Blossom, leaves	Trees/shrubs
Blossom	Flowers
Leaves	Spice, seasoning, flavoring
Blossom, branch/stem, leaves, seed/fruit	Trees/shrubs, vegetables, fruit
Blossom	Flowers
Root	Vegetables, fruit
Blossom, leaves	Flowers, herbs
Blossom	Flowers
Blossom/stem	Trees/shrubs
Blossom	Flowers
Blossom	Trees/shrubs
Blossom	Trees/shrubs
Blossom	Trees/shrubs
Blossom	Flowers
Blossom, leaves	Flowers, herbs, spice, seasoning, flavoring
Blossom, leaves	Herbs, spice, seasoning, flavoring
Blossom	Flowers
Blossom	Flowers
Blossom	Flowers
Blossom	Flowers
Blossom, leaves	Herbs, spice, seasoning, flavoring
Blossom	Flowers
Blossom	Flowers
Blossom	Flowers
Blossom	Flowers
Blossom	Flowers
Blossom	Flowers
Blossom	Vines
Blossom	Flowers
Blossom	Flowers

Harvesting and Drying

Harvesting Flowers for Drying

As the blooming cycles of flowers, herbs, and foliage progress, their colors, fragrances, and shapes go through a wide variety of change. Exactly when is the best time for harvesting is a difficult knowledge to acquire, but flowers are wonderful teachers. There are usually several flowers in different blooming stages at any given time, so you can experiment with drying the whole range, from fresh buds to mature flowers. Try to find the blooming cycle that produces everlastings with the best color and fragrance retention.

Remember that the real distinction between a dried flower and a fresh one is the absence of moisture. Flowers radiant with early-morning dew or glistening from rain drops should not be picked until mid-morning, when the dew has dried, or until the sun has dried the rain's moisture. Heavy rainstorms may leave flowers bruised for a day or two, but anticipate a new crop of blooms to arrive after the rain's nourishment.

When cutting flowers, allow a minimum of two inches of stem. Six to 12 inches is the best length for most flowers. If the stem allows, avoid side buds. With a low-growing plant whose blooms all mature at the same time, cutting the center stem is best. (Stems of this type, such as statice, are easier to dry with the hanging method because the growth pattern holds the flowers away from one another.) Larger plants or those with blooms maturing at the center and/or the top may be cut individually.

Heavy foliage should be removed before drying. Or, if the foliage is desirable, cut shorter stems and dry separately. To remove leaves from a stem, grip the stem below the bloom with one hand; with the fingers of your other hand pressed tight to the stem, pull stem up through your fingers.

Creating Perfect Everlastings

Since the everlasting floral gifts you make can only be as beautiful as the individual everlastings they're made from, it's important to invest some time learning about the changes that occur during the drying process. These changes, which take place during the transition from fresh-cut to completely dry, often involve color, shape, size, and strength, and will vary from flower to flower.

Color

Many flowers change color in the drying process, so you may have to experiment if you have a specific color in mind. Some red flowers will darken to purple or black, while others retain their bright color. Yellow flowers can change to gold, cream, or brown, while white flowers often take on a golden hue. The color in some flowers, such as the day lily, actually becomes translucent. Other flowers, such as hydrangea, retain their original colors.

Shapes

Changes in shape from fresh to dry can be strikingly different, and only experience can prevent surprise. Bay leaves maintain their shape perfectly, while others, such as geranium leaves, change from flat to curled. Queen Anne's lace, whose blossoms are full and upright when fresh, curves gently inward in its dried state.

Size

If you've ever come from the garden with a basket full of fresh-cut flowers and an imagination equally full of plans for a dozen everlasting bouquets, you no doubt understand about size changes during the drying process. Most flowers, leaves, and stems shrink as their moisture evaporates. Baby's breath, a long-time favorite of florists and brides, loses about 75% of its size during the drying process. With some flowers, however, such as lamb's ear and echinacea, the loss in size is barely noticeable.

Strength

Many flowers and herbs that appear strong before cutting often become quite delicate after drying. Daisy heads, for example, fall off very easily, and may need to be wired for support. Other plants, such as geranium, mint, and bay, are easily damaged when handled in their fresh state. So unless you plan to place your flowers under a protective glass dome, use sturdy flowers to fill out your bouquets and save the delicate ones for special accents.

Drying Methods

Hanging

The perfect location to hang flowers is warm, dry, and dark, with good air circulation. Air circulation, warmth, and dryness encourage moisture evaporation, while darkness prevents color fading.

To hang, combine six to 12 stems in a bundle, wrap together with twine, clothes clips, or a rubber band, and hang upside down. Always allow plenty of space between bundles for air circulation.

Check on the progress of your flowers often. Changes in shape, size, and color will surprise you. Some will be dramatic, some barely noticeable. Watch for buds that may or may not open. What happens to the leaves? Flowers with mildew or insect damage should be removed to prevent the damage from spreading.

Another reason to check flowers regularly is to prevent overdrying, which can ruin flowers. Drying times for some plants is three to four days if the environment is correct; other plants can require up to three weeks. Test for dryness by touching the flowers. If they're dry and rigid, they're ready. Gently shake your flower bundles, watching for shedding and listening for rustling sounds. When completely dry, flowers should be removed to a cool, dry location, away from direct sunlight.

Opposite page: A harvest of air-dried flowers and herbs can be stored close together in large bunches, whereas during the drying process they need considerable space between them for good air circulation.

Right: Silica gel crystals can be used alone or in combination with a microwave to dry flowers.

Desiccants

Desiccants are moisture-absorbing substances, such as sand, borax, cornmeal, and silica gel. Sand, the drying method used for centuries, takes several weeks and works best in dry climates. Borax or kitty litter also works well and a little faster than sand, but the weight of its granules can crush delicate flowers. Siliga gel is the most expensive but works fast, and its granules are very light. Many flowers also retain their colors better when dried with desiccants.

Choose a plastic or glass container (wood and cardboard allow moisture retention), and cover the bottom with an inch of desiccant. Place bell- and cup-shaped flowers on their sides, and other flowers face-up, with generous spacing in between. Gently cover the flowers with a layer of desiccant, being careful not to flatten their petals into unnatural positions. Experimenting is easy and results can be seen in as few as three or four days for delicate flowers, a week to ten days for flowers with thick or multiple petals. Flowers can be layered two or three rows deep in one container, but varieties should not be mixed unless drying times are known to be the same.

When removing the flowers, gently pour off the powder into an empty container. As the flowers come to the surface, carefully lift them out and set them aside. A small paintbrush can be used to whisk away any remaining powder residue on the petals. Attach a stem and they're ready to use.

Screens and Upright Drying

Other methods for air drying flowers are also quick and simple. Remove flower stems and place the flower head face-up on mesh wire or screening. Allow generous spacing to encourage air circulation. Calendula, chive blossoms, strawflower, amaranth, daisy, zinnia, and marigold dry well with this method. Separately dried stems are glued on after drying or created from wire if they won't show in your arrangement.

Some flowers dry well standing in a tall container. Juice cans, ventilated with holes in the sides and filled with about an inch of sand, are excellent choices. Baskets also work well as containers to dry flowers such as goldenrod, artemisia, mints, and grasses. Daffodils do well with this method, keeping their natural bow shape. Large-petaled flowers may droop if dried upright, giving them an exotic character that can add variety to an arrangement.

Glycerin

Baby's breath preserved with glycerin (far right) has a much fluffier appearance than air-dried baby's breath.

Many branches and leaves can be preserved with glycerin. Although their deep green colors will fade, the branches and leaves will be soft and pliable for for years. Make several diagonal slices in the stems and place them in a solution of three parts warm water to one part glycerin for about two weeks. Check the glycerin/ water mixture periodically for evaporation and replenish if necessary.

Microwave Drying

The microwave oven, used with silica gel, gives remarkable drying results. Moisture is removed during the oven's cooking process and then absorbed by the silica gel. Many of the general drying procedures described above apply to microwave drying: select specimens free from pests and blemishes; use flowers undampened by recent rain or dew; choose flowers in full bloom.

Begin by covering the bottom of a non-metal container with a thin layer of silica gel and arranging the flowers as directed in the desiccant section. Sprinkle silica gel between the petals and then cover them with more silica gel. If your microwave has settings from one through 10, put it on setting number four (about 300 watts); a microwave with three or four settings should be put on "half" (about 350 watts); and a microwave with "high" and "defrost" settings shoudl be put on "defrost" (about 200 watts).

Because there's so much variation in microwaves and in the amount of moisture a particular plant contains, it's impossible to predict exact drying times. Roughly, the drying time for one or more flowers or leaves in about ½ pound (300kg) of silica gel is 2 to 2½ minutes. The chart at right should give you some general guidelines, but do pick extra flowers for experimenting. A more exact method is to insert a non-metal thermometer into the silica gel and shut the oven off when it reaches the temperature indicated in the chart.

Flowers and leaves dried in the microwave will also need "standing time." For fragile flowers with only a few petals, the time is usually about ten minutes. Sturdy, heavy-petaled flowers can need up to 30 minutes. To prevent moisture from forming — and being reabsorbed into your flowers — put a lid on your container and leave it cracked just a bit. If you find your flowers are not dry enough after their standing time, they can be microwaved again for a short period.

Flower stems can also be dried in the microwave. Place five or six stems between a double layer of paper towels and cook for three to five minutes on the same setting you use for flowers. Check them after ten minutes of standing time, and return to the microwave if necessary.

Right: *Hydrangea dries well in the microwave.*

Microwave Drying Temperatures

Botanical Name	Common Name	Temperature	
Achillaea	Yarrow	160 F	70 C
Althea rosea	Hollyhock	150 F	65 C
Anemone	Windflower	140 F	60 C
Anthemum graveolens	Dill	150 F	65 C
Anthemis	Chamomile	160 F	70 C
Aquilegia	Columbine	160 F	70 C
Astilbe	Astilbe	160 F	70 C
Centaurea	Bachelor's button	150 F	65 C
Cystisus	Broom	160 F	70 C
Delphinium	Delphinium	170 F	75 C
Geum	Avens	150 F	65 C
Heuchera sanguinea	Coral bells	160 F	70 C
Hydrangea	Hydrangea	160 F	70 C
Iberis	Candytuft	150 F	65 C
Lupinus	Lupin	160 F	70 C
Narcissus	Daffodil	160 F	70 C
Rosa	Rose	170 F	75 C
Solidago	Goldenrod	160 F	70 C
Tagetes	Marigold	170 F	75 C
Veronica	Speedwell	170 F	75 C
Viola	Viola	150 F	65 C
Zinnia	Zinnia	170 F	75 C

Basic Floral Techniques

Colorful Everlastings

The gardens of the world offer such a variety of flowering plants that it's possible to find almost every flower color in nature. But if you're after a specific color and face time or climate limitations, there are several alternatives.

Commercially-dyed everlastings are available in many craft and floral supply stores. You may find their vibrant colors very appealing at first, but keep in mind that they often clash with the naturally soft colors of undyed materials.

Powdered dyes can be mixed with water to form a dye bath for air-dried flowers.

Flowers can also be lightened by adding bleach to a glycerin solution or soaking air-dried flowers in a bleach and water mixture. The branch of baby's breath on the left shows the natural color, while the branch on the right has been bleached.

You can add color to your own everlastings in several ways. A few drops of food coloring can be added to a glycerin solution (see page 20) and the color will be absorbed through the stems and into the flower petals. Many air-dried flowers can be soaked in a dye bath until the desired color is achieved and then hung upside down to dry again. Or you can add color with a light coat of spray paint. Whichever method you choose, realize that you will probably lose some flowers to experimentation.

Floral Wire

Floral wire is available in a variety of thicknesses and has many uses. Giving thought to the stems of your fresh flowers and the ways floral wire can improve them before drying can increase your arrangement possibilities. Heavy flowers, which can usually only support themselves on a short stem when dry, can be strengthened by wiring them when they are fresh. (In addition to providing strength, the wire also adds additional length to the stem.) Small flowers, whose stems are usually too weak to support a blossom when dry, can be supported by replacement stems made from wire. Floral wire can also be used to create curves in once-straight stems.

There is no single best way to wire a flower. The method you choose should complement the individual characteristics of your flower and the way you plan to use it. If you're making a nosegay, for instance, and the flowers you've chosen have bulky stems, you can make insertion into the base much easier by removing the flowers' stems while they're fresh and replacing them with wire stems.

Supporting Flower Heads With Wire

Many popular dried flowers, such as echinacea and zinnia, tend to re-absorb moisture in humid areas, causing them to become limp and droop. The best way to prevent these flowers from wilting is to support their petals with floral wire, as described below.

This same technique can be used to prevent heavy flower petals from curving downwards during the drying process.

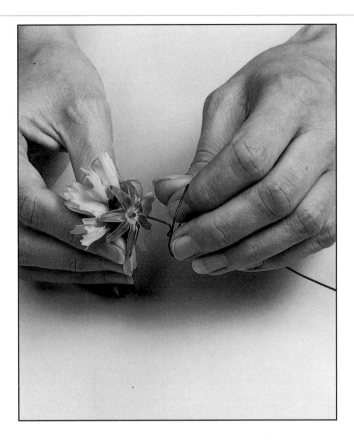

1. Bend the top of a length of medium-gauge floral wire into a spiral that's slightly smaller than the flower. Bend the remaining wire (the stem) at a right angle so that it is perpendicular to the spiral.

2. Bend the spiral's tip so that it points parallel with the wire stem.

3. Holding the flower gently but securely between your thumb and forefinger, insert the pointed end of the spiral through the back of the flower where the stem used to be.

   Continue pressing the wire through the flower until you see it come through the front. Gently push down on the flower until the wire spiral touches the petals. Now turn the flower right side up; it should sit firmly on the wire stem and the petals should hide the spiral.

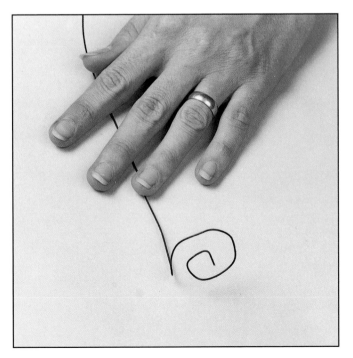

Replacing A Bulky Stem With Wire

Flowers like centurea (pictured), strawflower, and zinnia benefit by adding wire stems when they're fresh. This technique also works well with some cones, pods and fruits.

1. Cut the stem 4 to 6 inches (10 to 15 cm) below the flower. Flowers with bulky stems or large heads will need a piece of heavy-gauged wire; fine- or medium-gauged wire works fine with most other flowers.
2. Place one end of the wire at the end of the stem and apply enough pressure to push the wire up through the stem and the blossom. (Tip: apply pressure to the wire, not the flower.)
3. Continue pushing the wire until you have several inches of wire above the blossom.

    Now form a U-shaped hook in the wire. Hold the stem just below the blossom and gently pull the wire back down into the petals until the hook anchors in the head of the flower and is invisible. Trim wire to length desired for stem.

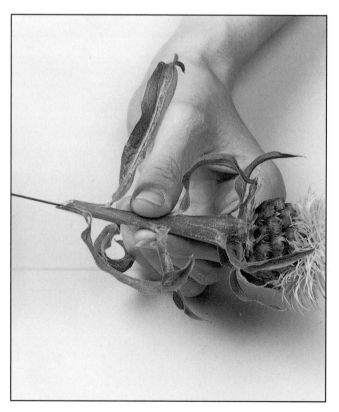

Using Floral Wire to Curve A Stem And/Or Add Strength

Floral wire can also be used to add support to a long-stemmed flower and to form curved stems.

1. Hold both the wire and the stem of a fresh flower near the top ends. Insert the top end of the wire horizontally into the stem for about an inch. This piece of inserted wire will be anchored in place as the stem shrinks around it during the drying process.
2. Hold the flower and the wire below the point of insertion and begin wrapping the wire around the stem until you reach the end, being careful not to crush the stem or lower blossoms.
3. If you want a curved stem, allow your wired flower to soften or wilt a little and then gently bend the stem into the desired curve. Stand or hang to dry as usual.

Lengthening And/Or Strengthening A Stem Without Wire

If your wired flower stems will show in the everlasting gift you're making, or if you just have a preference for natural stems, you can lengthen and/or strengthen a stem simply by borrowing a stem from another plant.

1. Flower stems come in all sizes and strengths. Far left: this thick, hollow stem is unable to support its heavy blossom. Far right: this narrow stem is too weak to support even a small blossom after drying. Center: a tough, narrow stem (goldenrod) and a stiff, hollow stem (wild weed) have been cut to desired lengths.

2. Insert the tough, narrow stem into the weak, hollow stem; likewise, insert the narrow, weak stem into the stiff, hollow stem. As the flowers dry, natural shrinkage will secure the two stems together. After drying, cut the bottom of the stem at a sharp angle for easier insertion into your base.

Floral Tape

Floral tape is simple to use and is available in a multitude of colors and widths. The tape is most commonly used to camouflage wired or fake stems, but it can also be used to strengthen stems, to join several stems together, or to add leaves to bare stems.

Begin with your tape at a slight angle so it will overlap as you wrap it down the stem. Apply enough tension on the tape to stretch it slightly. When you reach the bottom of the stem or floral pick, cut the tape and roll the end between your fingers to seal.

Floral Picks

Floral picks are used to make insertion into a base faster and less damaging to everlastings. The wooden picks available in craft and floral supply stores come in a variety of lengths and are usually painted green. The top of the pick has a short length of thin-gauge floral wire attached to it, while the bottom of the pick is cut to a sharp point. You may also come across metal picks shaped like hair pins and staples, and many inventive designers have been known to make their own floral picks with toothpicks and thread or yarn.

A large flower can be wired to a pick alone, or a bouquet of smaller everlastings can be arranged and picked as a bundle. Flowers can be picked before or after drying, but the wire should be secured tighter around fresh flowers to allow for shrinkage during drying.

How To Pick A Single Stem

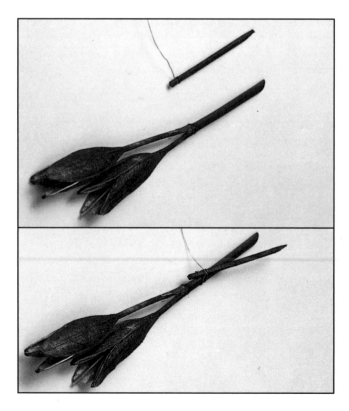

The technique described below can also be used to pick bows, cones, pods, and craft novelties.

1. Hold the stem and the pick together, making sure there's enough stem to reach the top of the pick and that the flower is above the wire.
2. Begin tightly wrapping the wire around the stem and the pick. Make several extra turns with the wire at the point where the wire connects with the pick.
3. Continue spiraling the wire down the stem until the wire ends. If desired, clip the stem at the end of the wire so the pick will perforate your base easier.

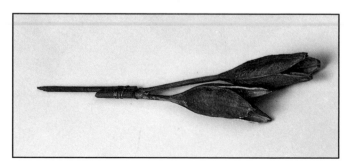

How To Pick A Bundle

1. Arrange your selected materials (flowers, herbs, greenery, or any combination thereof) as you would a small bouquet. Clip the stems even at the bottom.
2. Hold the bouquet with the stems pressed together near the mid-point of the stem.
3. Attach the pick as directed above.

Foam

Floral foam is one of the most flexible design tools for creating everlasting floral gifts. The foam can be purchased in a variety of pre-cut shapes (cones and balls are shown here), or you can buy large blocks and cut it to the exact shape you need with a serrated knife.

Flowers with tough, angular-cut stems can be inserted directly into the foam, while flowers with weak stems may need to be wired or picked first.

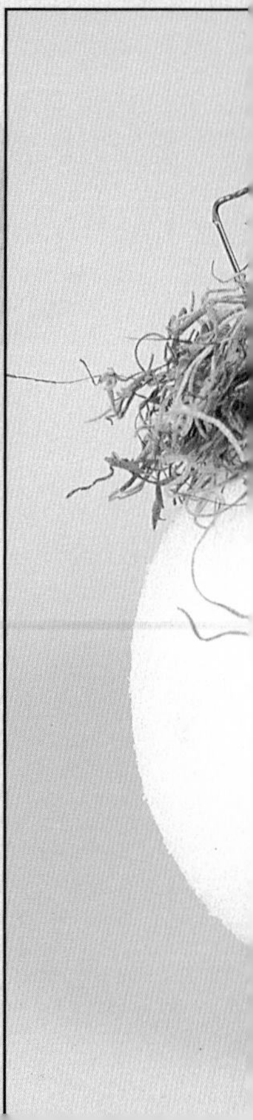

Pins and Mosses

Most floral designers choose to cover their floral foam with moss before inserting flowers to prevent bare foam from disrupting the natural look of the design.

A variety of mosses can be purchased at floral and craft supply stores or gathered outdoors. If you choose to gather your own moss, you may need to microwave it for a few minutes to kill any small insects living in the moss.

Moss can be attached to floral foam with floral pins, water-based glue, or hot glue. Since many foams will melt when exposed to hot glue, it's a good idea to test a small area of your foam before you begin.

Glue Guns

Some floral designers view glue guns as an essential tool of the trade, while other designers get by just fine without them. Lightweight "mini glue guns" are usually available in craft supply stores for under ten dollars, and they do offer a quick, simple way to adhere items.

The adhesive glue used in glue guns is much stronger than the water-based glues used by school children, and you may be surprised at the wide variety of items—such as pine cones, nuts, and craft novelties—that can be hot-glued.

Working Tips:

- While your glue gun is heating up, spread a protective layer of newspaper over your work area. If your glue gun does not have a stand, find a glass plate or other non-flammable item to rest it on.
- Hold larger items in place for at least a minute after gluing to ensure proper bonding. Extremely large or heavy items may need to be attached with heavy-gauged wire and then hot-glued for reinforcement.
- You may notice strands of glue that resemble spider webs on your flowers. Don't worry about them as you're working—they'll easily pull off later.
- Apply glue to flower stems, not petals.
- When working with floral foam, test a small surface of the foam to make sure the hot glue won't melt it. If melting does occur, use floral greening pins to cover the foam with moss and then glue the floral materials to the moss.

Safety Tips:

- Keep a bowl of ice water near your work area in case of burns.
- Do not leave an unsupervised child near a glue gun.
- Unplug your glue gun as soon as you've finished using it.

Gift Packing

If you're shipping or mailing an everlasting gift . . .

When preparing your box, keep in mind that your package—and its delicate contents—will not be treated delicately en route and the beauty you've created will be destroyed if packaged improperly.

First, gently wrap your gift in a sheet of floral paper, waxed side facing the gift. (Tissue paper also works well, but doesn't have the protective benefit of a wax coating.) Crumple up several more sheets of floral paper and use them to cushion indentations and delicate areas of your gift. Secure these paper cushions with a large sheet of floral paper wrapped and taped around the gift.

Then fill the bottom of a box at least three times larger than your wrapped gift with crumpled newspaper or other shipping material. Gently place your gift in the center, and fill the gaps beside and above the gift with more crumpled paper.

When finished, close the box and shake it. If you hear any movement you know you've packed the box too loosely.

If you're hand-delivering an everlasting gift . . .

Wrap the gift in floral paper (waxed side towards the gift) and tie with a ribbon. If you'd prefer to wrap the gift in regular wrapping paper, pre-wrap it in at least four sheets of floral paper first to prevent damage from the abrasiveness of stiff paper.

Garlands and Swags

Traditionally used as holiday decorations for staircases, doorways, and fireplaces, today's garlands are at home in all rooms of the house in every season. Thin, delicate garlands can be shaped around mirrors, chandeliers, and furniture or on serving tables at weddings and parties.

Most garlands are made by attaching flowers and greenery to a length of straight wire that serves as a base. This wire can be gently bent or curved to a special shape after all of the dried materials have been attached. There are several ways to secure your everlastings to the base wire, and you should choose the one with which you are most comfortable and also suits the plant materials you've chosen.

Method #1: A single base wire is looped around each bundle several times and then returned to its original straight position. Each successive bundle should cover the wire loops from the previous bundle.

Method #2: A long length of medium-gauged wire is secured to the wire base and looped around both the flower bundle and the base wire. As with the previous method, each successive bundle should cover the wire loops from the previous bundle.

Method #3: Small bunches of flowers and/or greenery can be wired together into bundles before being attached to the garland's base, or the stems of each small bundle can be held tightly together against the wire base with the left hand while the right hand secures it to the base with wire.

Opposite Page

A spool of fine-gauged jeweler's wire was used to secure small bunches of everlastings to a length of medium-gauged floral wire. The flowers include: dianthus, oak leaf hydrangea, caspia, annual statice, gypsophila, pearly everlasting, roses, globe amaranth, Dutch iris, sweet Annie, German statice, lavender, silver king artemisia, boxwood, sage, love-in-a-mist, and dyed wild grasses. Colorful ribbon streamers were inserted through a loop made in the ends of the wire.

Right: *This delicate chandelier garland was made by braiding several ribbons through a garland of springeri fern and hot-gluing roses, pepper grass, and stock into the ferns.*

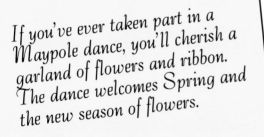

If you've ever taken part in a Maypole dance, you'll cherish a garland of flowers and ribbon. The dance welcomes Spring and the new season of flowers.

Below: *This pastel fireplace swag uses a base of copper wire with a background of silver king artemisia. Accent flowers include larkspur, hydrangea, roses, pearly everlasting, strawflowers, celosia, globe amaranth, carnations, German statice, and pepper grass.*

Right: *Small bundles of flowers were alternately wired with small bundles of ferns to a stout length of green macrame cord. The flowers include roses, rabbit tobacco, ti tree, gypsophila, statice, and strawflowers.*

Swags are simply bouquets of flowers, herbs, or greenery that have been wired together near the base of the stems and are displayed upside down. Large swags may need to be wired in small bunches that are then secured with more wire. Bows or other decorations are generally wired or hot-glued to the top of the swag to cover any bare wires.

Above: A full bouquet of baby's breath makes a lovely swag that can change with the seasons by changing bows.

Far left: A Halloween swag made from wheat stalks and an orange plaid bow was decorated with glycerin-preserved oak leaves, German statice, and craft novelties that were hot-glued under the bow.

Left: A wire stem of artificial berries adds holiday cheer to a swag of bearded wheat.

This swag of Caribbean flowers was made from a bouquet of rattlesnake ginger, helani tulip ginger, mink protea, wheat calathea, and Chinese fan palms. The soft curves in the bow were achieved by using French ribbon, which is lined with several rows of thin wire that help maintain curves and shapes.

Following Scandinavian tradition, walls are decked with swags made of grain sheaves brought in at harvest and shared at Christmas with family and friends. This keeps the goddess of grain alive through the winter.

Opposite Page

A swag of dyed ti tree flowers and greenery was first adorned with a large plaid bow. Small sprigs of tinted baby's breath were then hot-glued under the bow as a special touch.

Above left: This fragrant, traditional apple swag was made by threading dried apples, fresh nutmegs, Spartan roses, bay leaves, and dried peppers through a tapestry needle onto a length of ribbon.

Prepare the apples by first peeling and slicing them, taking care to remove any seeds to avoid worms. Sprinkle with sea salt and allow to dry on a piece of window screening for about ten days. The nutmegs were prepared by drilling a small hole through them and the bay leaves had holes punched in them before threading. (Note: the apples may swell and shrink as the humidity changes, but this will not hurt the swag.)

Above right: Small wreath bases of straw were tied together with raffia and decorated with dried peppers and herbs.

Larger, more permanent garlands may need the support of a wooden base. The base for the garland shown here was cut with a band saw from ½″ (1¾ cm) plywood and covered with felt using a spray adhesive.

The base was then outlined with a row of glycerin-preserved cedar attached with hot glue. The wheat bouquets were arranged next and secured in place with staples and hot glue.

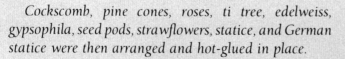

Cockscomb, pine cones, roses, ti tree, edelweiss, gypsophila, seed pods, strawflowers, statice, and German statice were then arranged and hot-glued in place.

Tip: Determine how you will be hanging the garland (i.e. hooks, screws, etc.) before you begin decorating the base.

Wreaths

Wreaths have existed in some form since the ancient cultures of Persia, Parthia, and Artemia. Today their popularity is rapidly increasing as more and more people realize their versatility and beauty.

Every wreath will need a base of some sort. You can choose from a variety of bases in craft supply stores or you can make your own bases inexpensively at home.

Flowers can be picked into a base alone or in small bunches, and should be inserted at an angle deep enough to secure the pick in place and to cover the exposed portion of the pick. Continue inserting picked flowers into the base in the same direction, overlapping the materials so that the flowers from each new insertion cover the area where the previous pick was inserted.

Flowers can also be attached to a moss-covered base by placing a small amount of hot glue on their stems and inserting them into the moss. As with picking, always insert the flowers at an angle, and maintain that same angle all the way around the wreath.

Some designers like to cover their wreath base with a background material they have in abundance—such as artemisia, German statice, or baby's breath—and then add spots of color with their more precious everlastings. Other designers choose to cover the inner and outer edges of the wreath base with one type of everlasting and then fill in the middle area with everlastings in a variety of shapes, texture, and color. Other less structured methods of designing wreaths often yield equally beautiful results, so don't be afraid to let your flowers dictate their own designs.

Left: Insert flowers into the base at the same angle all the way around the wreath.

Right: Straw bases, vine bases (grape, wisteria, and honeysuckle), and wire bases. Bases can also be made from styrofoam, pressboard, and heavy cardboard.

Below left: To make a vine base, hold several lengths of vine together and bend to form a circle. The circular shape can be secured by wrapping the vine with a thinner piece of vine or with spool wire.

Note: the vines must be "pliable" in order to form a circular shape without splitting. A vine's pliability depends on several factors: the growing season in which it was cut; how old the plant is; how long ago it was cut; and recent temperatures and humidity. You may have some success in softening stiff vines by soaking them in warm water until they soften.

Below center: To make a moss base, attach a length of yarn securely to a pre-formed wire ring and then place moss around the wire form. Secure the moss to the form by wrapping the yarn around the form. The moss should be firm when you've finished.

Below right: To make a straw base, form a circle from heavy, stiff wire and twist the ends together. Attach a length of spool wire (heavy gauge) to the wire circle and begin placing handsful of straw against the form and wrapping them together with the spool wire. The straw should be firm when you've finished.

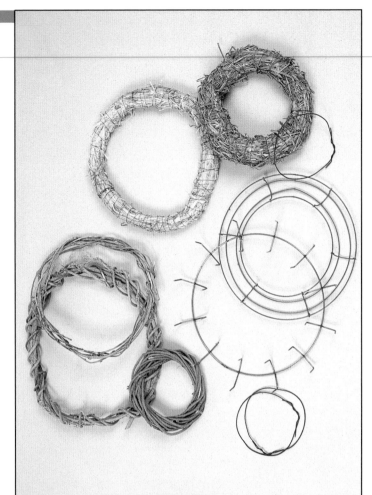

Lantana's orange-gold signifies victory, luck, prosperity, and even supramental qualities. Add ivy for lasting attachment and a pinch of modesty, and you have a lucky rabbit's foot in the shape of a wreath.

Yellow statice sinuata and strawflower, orange and gold lantana are highlighted by the blue of globe thistle and green ivy leaves. Filled in with white statice, some pink from chive blossoms and yarrow, this makes a fine all occasion gift to cheer the spirits and brighten the home.

Right: *Lavender for its fragrance and traditional uses for cleanliness, with rosemary for purity, tansy, yarrow, bay and box for strength, remembrance, health and longevity are part of this intriguing wreath of myth and lore.*

Below: *Ivy twines around excelsior like it twined centuries ago up lampposts. Taverns along the coach lines displayed ivy on their signs to signify that spirits, alcoholic beverages, were served inside.*

Both of these wreaths can be made with fresh-cut flowers and greenery and will dry naturally over time. You may wish to cover the base more densely than usual to prevent bare spots from showing as natural shrinkage occurs.

Though plain and simple on the surface, there is power, fortitude, grace, serenity, abundance, and prosperity deep within the historical backgrounds of money plant, Job's tears, iris pods, oregano, and cardoon.

Top left: *Job's tear, seed pods, Fuller's teasel, and wild grasses were first arranged in small bouquets, wired together, and then wired to a wreath base of wisteria vine. (The wire was wrapped with brown floral tape so it would blend in with the base.)*

Bottom left: *A heart-shaped grapevine base was decorated with roses, pine cones, ribbons, caspia, statice, and wild mint. The flowers were hot-glued first, with the pine cones and caspia glued in last.*

The base was made by grouping six to eight lengths of grapevine together and securing them on one end with wire. With the wired end facing downward, the grapevines were split into two equal sections and curved around to form the heart shape.

When the two sides come back together at the bottom of the heart, secure them together with wire and trim the dangling vines to a length you find pleasing. Be sure to cover the wire with ribbons, moss, or flowers while decorating.

Branches of birch were first wired to a grapevine wreath base. A small square of styrofoam was then wired to the branches and covered with moss, heather, pepper grass, eucalyptus, plurosa ferns, and elephant ear pods were then picked into the foam. As a special touch, small pieces of spanish moss were hot-glued inside the elephant ear pods to imitate a bird's nest.

Opposite Page

Top left: *Thin branches from a willow tree were cut in the early spring (when the branches were still supple) to form the base for this wreath. An assortment of mosses and tree fungi were then hot-glued in place.*

Top right: *The natural beauty of excelsior makes a lovely background material for this unusual wreath. The excelsior was first secured to a wire ring with twine and then decorated with a large bouquet made from golden-rod, hydrangea, rabbit tobacco, wild grasses, and artemisia. The flowers were inserted into the excelsior with picks.*

Bottom left: *A bouquet of roses, hyssop, delphinium, sage, and cardamon leaves was first wired together and then attached with wire to a moss base. Single accent flowers were then added to the top of the wreath with a water-based glue.*

Bottom right: *A heart-shaped straw base was first covered with an assortment of colorful porpourri and single flowers were then glued among the potpourri. Both the potpourri and the flowers were attached with a water-based glue.*

Evergreens are synonymous with longevity. As they grow, seemingly for centuries, they have come to represent perpetual vitality. The endearing gift of endurance can be shared with a friend by giving a wreath of evergreens.

Left: *Fragrant cardamon and fraser fir, along with artemisia, holly, rose hips, passion flowers, boxwood, white pine, rhododendron, heather, and Russian sage, were clustered together into small bouquets and picked into a straw base.*

Center: *Clusters of roses, Mexican sunflowers, statice, celosia, and pussy willows were first hot-glued to a grapevine base. As other summer garden flowers bloomed, they were dried and hot-glued randomly to the wreath for a patchwork effect.*

Below: *A background of glycerin-preserved fraser fir was first picked into a styrofoam base. Wired pinon pine cones were added next, and then sprigs of sweet Annie. Last, small pieces of caspia were hot-glued into the fir branches and the large bow was wired in place.*

To celebrate a promotion, give a wreath of royal blue and purple. The intrinsic value of these flowers that adorn the statice bears a message that says "good work" and "all continues well."

These miniature wreaths are made from a base of fragrant sweet Annie (annual artemisia) and make wonderful small gifts.

The bases are made by twisting long stems of sweet Annie around medium-gauged wire and then wrapping with sewing thread to secure. Bases can also be made from short pieces of sweet Annie by forming small bunches and securing them to a small metal ring with thin-gauged wire.

The bases can be pre-made and stored until a special occasion occurs, and then quickly decorated with small, meaningful flowers.

Opposite Page

Clusters of statice latifolia were first picked into a straw base to form the background for these colorful everlastings. The grey is artemisia; the blue is salvia; and the violet is globe amaranth.

Left: *The traditional Christmas colors in this wreath were formed with somewhat untraditional Christmas everlastings: celosia, heather, statice, boxwood, roses, and cockscomb. All of the materials were hot-glued to a vine base.*

Opposite Page

Small Christmas ornaments were arranged and hot-glued to a straw base with German statice, caspia, sumac, globe amaranth, and statice.

Right: *This culinary wreath was made by hot-gluing peppers, statice, mint, bay leaves, garlic cloves, cinnamon, nuts, sumac, eucalpytus, and bows to a vine base. The wreath is quick to make and will remain fragrant for many months.*

Little angels 'mid the herbs smile approvingly on the soothing sumac. Long ago, sumac was used for winter ailments. The wild grape lends charity through its vine, forming the base of this wreath for Christmas giving.

Opposite Page

Top left: Ironweed, lamb's ear, German statice, ammobium, baby's breath, artemisia, and feverfew were picked together in small bunches and inserted into a straw base.

Top right: Clusters of bright color decorate the soft tones of this straw-based wreath. The flowers include: German statice, goldenrod, globe amaranth, salvia, yarrow, sage, artemisia, and statice sinuata.

Bottom left: Money plant, daffodils, grasses, rabbit tobacco, heather, and Jerusalem sage were picked into a straw base.

Bottom right: This wreath was made by wiring flowers to a length of medium-gauged wire and then joining the two wire ends together to form a circle. (See **Garlands and Swags** for more detailed directions.) The everlastings include: pepper grass, sweet Annie, iris, pearly everlasting, wild yarrow, lamb's ear, annual statice, sea statice, wormwood, artemisia persiana, sage, azaleas, blue salvia, dusty miller berries, and anise hyssop.

Potpourris, Sachets and Pomanders

A potpourri, by definition, is a fragrant mixture of dried flowers and/or herbs. They can be made from whole petals and leaves or from much smaller pieces. Potpourris often use non-fragrant flowers to make them more decorative, and this lack of fragrance can be compensated for by adding concentrated, scented oils.

The potpourris in this chapter were formed with naturally fragrant flowers and leaves whose historical meanings make them ideal gifts for special occasions.

In their finely-ground form, potpourris can be used to make sachets, pomanders, and other fragrant gifts.

Left: *The range of pinks and reds are as pleasing as the fragrance of rose for a gift of love on Valentine's Day.*
Peppermint geranium leaves, Tijuana bronze geranium leaves, scented geranium flowers, fuschia blossoms, impatiens, roses, oil of roses.

Above: *For a variety of color and fragrance when flower ingredients lack their own, try adding tiny colored hearts of scented wax or shavings from a bar of your favorite scented soap.*
Upper: *Statice latifolia, achillea paprika, myrica pennsylvanica leaves, pink wax hearts (scented).*
Lower: *Salvia farinacea, salvia leucantha (all purple), santolina, coreopsis, feverfew, lavender, delphinium.*

On cutting board: *Cinnamon sticks, cloves, nutmeg, star anise.*

#1: *Create a tangy lemon simmer with lemon balm, lemon grass, lemon verbena, lemon-scented geranium leaves, sassafras, and lemon thyme.*

#2: *Friendship and love lore are combined in this sweetly scented potpourri made entirely from geranium leaves. It will linger in the air as memories of love linger in the mind.*

#3: *Bay leaves and peppers make a crisp and fragrant potpourri, great for a stovetop simmer . . . or add to Cajun dishes, meatloaf, spaghetti, etc.*

#4: Beastie Feastie: *A potpourri of dried apple seed pods, beans, nuts, and berries are pretty to keep by a window or on the porch for over-wintering birds and critters to find.*

#5: *For a refreshing bath, add these mints as the water fills the tub. Excellent teas can be brewed directly from this mix, or by adding a pinch to other teas for gentle steeping, and strain before serving.*

Mountain mint, apple mint, spearmint.

#6: *To Christmas scents of blue spruce, white pine, fraser fir, cryptomera, and heather, add a drop of oil of rosemary for a mystery fragrance that will captivate guests.*

#7: *A simmer supreme to bring the ski slope and mountain air indoors with a tangy oriental flavor as mystical as a foggy evening.*

Cedar, lemon balm, sage, star anise, tansy, mint, cardamon, annua, bay.

#8: Golden Wedding Anniversary: *Ghost wormwood, yellow strawflower, oregano palchellium, feverfew, santolina, salvia farinacea (white), oil of honeysuckle.*

#9: Silver Wedding Anniversary: *Salvia farinacea (white), Queen Anne's lace, Roman wormwood, artemisia stelleriana, ivy, lambs ear, statice latifolia, pearly everlasting, oil of rose.*

#10: English Honeymoon Keepsake Potpourri: *Nigella, heather, lavender, wild rose, elsholtzia, mint, oil of lavender, oil of vanilla.*

#11: Mother's Day: *Love in a mist, veronica, rose, pansy, rhododendron, geranium, broom, carnations, astilbe, lupine, oil of violet.*

#12: Wedding — Marriage Everlastingly: *Variegated ivy, sage, pearly everlasting, sassafras, lemon verbena, baby's breath, statice sinuata, globe amaranth, boxwood, statice latifolia, oil of honeysuckle, oil of sweet orange orris.*

Potpourri ingredients bespeak the lore of an era when the unknown was magical.

#1: *Straw and moss ensure a strong, healthy family staying close to home.*

Corn, peas, star anise, and cinnamon bring protection and prosperity. Add oil of vanilla.

#2: *For money and prosperity in worldly riches, combine cloves, clover, goldenrod, honeysuckle, dried peas, rice, sassafras, money plant, and oil of sweet orange.*

#3: *Tying knots or making balls of grass to keep in the home protect it from harm by nature. Rosemary protects the home and persons within from illness. Flavor with oil of rosemary.*

#4: *Queen Anne's lace and sage bring wisdom in trying times. Clover and cardamon bring courage and peaceful thoughts. Flavor with oil of violet.*

#5: *Lady's mantle acts as a protective cover. Add some fragrance with oil of wisteria and oil of bitter almond. Carry a bit with you when traveling.*

#6: *As ivy clings and holly warns away, seek refuge where they abide. The everlasting wintergreen emits an oil that will enliven this potpourri.*

#7: *Restful sleeping on a little pillow filled with lavender will soothe the spirit with sweet dreams of love and happiness.*

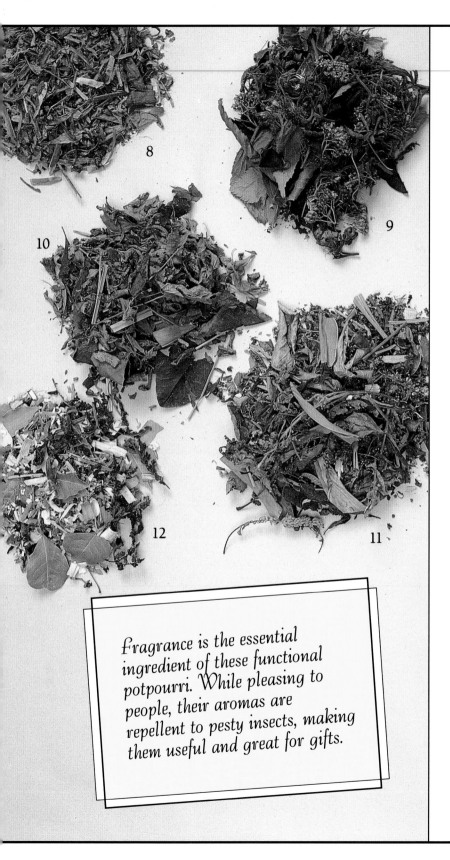

#8: *Marigold, tansy, wormwood, santolina, and nicotiana will ward off pests. Place this potpourri in trunks, closets, suitcases, or the attic.*

#9: *Angelica, comfrey, chamomile, viburnum, lavender, and yarrow soothe the tired feet. Use as a soak for reviving the souls.*

#10: *Sassafras, lemon verbena, rosemary, southernwood, sage, and ivy, with oil of sweet orange, are a blend of favorites especially for linen.*

#11: *Sandlewood, lemon verbena, cedar, star anise, cardamon, lemon grass, oregana, milkweed, and artemisia annua will freshen the air like a tropical forest.*

#12: *Bay leaves, cedar chips, and tansy leaves will comfort your pet when put in a sack and placed near or within their bedding.*

Fragrance is the essential ingredient of these functional potpourri. While pleasing to people, their aromas are repellent to pesty insects, making them useful and great for gifts.

#1 *This potpourri of good luck, prosperity, wisdom, happiness, and protection makes a meaningful gift on Graduation Day.*

Goldenrod, poppy, globe amaranth, statice, money plant, geranium, santolina, wormwood, yarrow, pansy, lantana, oil of wisteria, oil of sweet orange, orris.

#2: *The classic Victorian potpourri includes:*

Wild pink roses, statice latifolia, lady's mantle, fern, heather, ivy, lupine, impatiens, bouganvilla, strawflower, oil of rose, oil of bitter almond, orris.

#3: *A nostalgic potpourri from your Hawaiian vacation will help relieve jet lag.*

Coleus, tiger lily, pansy, calendula, globe amaranth, day lily, celosia, cardamon, rosemary, salvia, sedum, statice, marigold, daisy, delphinium, coreopsis, broom, geranium, oil of coconut, oil of bayberry, oil of sweet orange.

#4: *After the Christmas tree is up, the wreaths are hung, and the staircase is swagged, guest gifts can be made from the evergreen remnants. Even though they will bronze like autumn leaves, their scent will last until next Christmas.*

Boxwood, white pine, fraser fir, yellow pine, chamesyparis, heather, blue spruce.

5

4

6

#5: *Our traditional red, white, and blue for holidays like May Day, July Fourth, Veterans Day, Memorial Day, and Flag Day can be celebrated indoors with:*

Salvia (white), delphinium (blue), sumac (red), cardamon, cinnamon stick, oil of rosemary, oil of vanilla.

#6: *Enjoy these riches at Thanksgiving:*

Ivy, poppy, wormwood, sumac, oakleaf hydrangea, peppers, oil of bitter almond, whole cloves, nutmeg.

#1: *Laze in the summer shade with the hot colors of this patio potpourri.*

Bouganvilla, delphinium, geranium, heather, yarrow (white), statice, Maltese cross, yarrow (pink), bee balm, ivy, elderberry, oil of bayberry, oil of vanilla.

#2: *The fading glory of summer sun sets the trees ablaze with copper and gold. This potpourri brings the glow indoors, and scents the air with fall's crispness.*

Lemon verbena, sassafras, statice, marigold, coreopsis, foxglove, pansy, lemon grass, yarrow, oil of rosemary, orris.

#3: *Chilling winter whites with a lingering touch of autumn sun show in the flowers here, while oil of violet hints at spring.*

Hydrangea, wormwood, lavender, silver king, lambs ear, santolina, elsholtzia, mountain mint, rabbit tobacco, horehound, artemisia annua, oil of violet.

#4: *Spring is greening grass, daffodils, and birds calling. We anticipate the buds, and plant zinnias by the mailbox. This potpourri invites new sweetness and longer days.*

Variegated grass, foxglove, wild rose, clover, eumonius, sweet pea, pansy, salvia, oil of honeysuckle.

> The poppy represents joy in nature. With its cheerful orange color, it conveys the quality of courage. This dry flower pot-pourri makes a fitting gift in autumn to cheer one through the long winter months.

5

6

7

#5: *A fresh and dry mix for fragrance and color, these holiday greens and reds can be carried to a party or placed in a basket by the reading lamps.*

Dry: *Red roses, red Maltese cross, red rose geraniums.*

Fresh: *Ivy leaves, magnolia, holly, bay leaves, heuchera, oil of evergreen, oil of vanilla.*

#6: *This three-fold item can be a potpourri gift, an air freshener (with oil of wintergreen added), or a message of love, with its magnolia, ivy, baby's breath, sumac, and the ethereal night bloom of cyris.*

#7: *Memories of Christmases past make the holidays special. Here are evergreens, now bronze, with some pods and small cones. Add cinnamon sticks, moss, sumac, and a drop of oil of bayberry, and you can give a gift of remembrance.*

Through the centuries spices and fragrant flowers have been collected, displayed, revered, and even used as currency. Their aromas are treasured all over the world, and gifts made from them are both fragrant and decorative.

Traditionally, sachets were filled with spices, dried flowers, and/or herbs that were ground to the consistency of fine powder, although today many sachet bags are filled with plant materials not much smaller than those found in potpourris.

Once you've made a fragrant sachet or potpourri, you may wish to add decorative touches with small pieces of ribbon and everlastings that easily attach with hot glue.

Left: *Cinnamon, cloves, mace, nutmeg, allspice and orris.*

Top: *Styrofoam egg shapes (plastic also works well) were covered with sheet moss, covered lightly with hot glue, and rolled in lavender potpourri for a fragrant holiday decoration.*

Bottom: *Pomanders decorated with ribbons, everlastings, and pearls make fragrant Christmas tree ornaments.*

Ingredients: ground cinnamon, clove, mace, and nutmeg; one bottle of applesauce.

Mix equal amounts of the ground spices in a glass bowl. Strain the applesauce for about 30 minutes to remove excess water. Add just enough applesauce to the spice mixture to form the consistency of cookie dough. Mold the dough into balls, bells, pears, eggs, or any other shape you desire. Place on wax paper and allow to dry for approximately three weeks. (Humid weather will lengthen the drying time.) Decorate with ribbons, lace, cloth, or everlastings.

Opposite Page

Top left: *These Victorian-styled keepsake hearts were filled with delicate potpourri. They can be used to hold jewelry pins, decorate a bedroom dresser, or scent a lingerie drawer.*

Bottom left: *A white doily was folded in half, filled with a bag of potpourri, and woven together with colorful ribbon. Tradition holds that this potpourri's ingredients—wormwood and sweet woodruff—repel moths.*

Left: *Potpourri kissing balls were traditional decorations for Victorian holidays. The kissing ball shown here was made by first covering a styrofoam ball with sheet moss. The moss was then covered with a thin layer of hot-glue and rolled in potpourri. After the glue dried, lace ribbons were tied around the ball.*

Top: *To make a gift sachet, fill a bag of soft netting or tulle with potpourri and insert it into a decorative fabric bag, pouch, or pillow.*

Bottom: *These potpourri bags were tied with ribbons and adorned with everlastings that were hot-glued in place.*

Topiaries and Trees

Topiaries and trees are a creative and fun way to make everlasting floral gifts. They can be displayed on the floor, next to a bookcase or in a lighted corner, or placed on a table or shelf for a unique centerpiece.

Like wreaths and garlands, the base of a topiary or tree can be covered with a single background material or covered with a variety of colors and shapes. And because they're made with a styrofoam base, it's simple to change bows, ribbons, and select flowers to reflect a particular holiday or season.

Topiaries are built by inserting the top end of a stem into a styrofoam ball or cone base, and the bottom end of the stem into a block of floral foam or a flower pot filled with plaster of Paris. Your topiary's stem can be a natural branch, a cinnamon stick, or a thin metal pipe that's concealed with moss, ribbon, or glycerin-preserved leaves.

Cut the top end of your topiary's stem at a sharp angle so it won't damage the styrofoam base when it's inserted. Some designers prefer to decorate the styrofoam base of the topiary first, and then insert the stem; while others prefer to add their everlastings only after the base is firmly anchored on the stem. (Note: The latter method works best if you are working with especially delicate flowers.)

Left: This double topiary is an exciting variation that uses the same basic construction technique as a single topiary. The flowers were attached with hot glue and include hydrangea, strawflowers, larkspur, daisies, cockscomb, aster, German statice, globe amaranth, pepper berries, and sumac.
Opposite Page
Top left: Use floral pins to cover your base with moss.
Top right: Secure the stem and the tree base in an upright position.
Bottom: Insert single or clustered flowers into the base with picks, or hot-glue flower heads and small stems into the moss.

Preservation and Care

The beauty of topiaries and trees, like all everlasting gifts, can last for years if treated with care. Some tips to remember:

Exposure to direct sunlight will cause fading, so never display an arrangement on a windowsill or other sunny area.

Many dried flowers will re-absorb moisture and lose their shape when exposed to damp locations, so avoid displaying everlastings in the bathroom or near the stove.

Spray your arrangements once a year with ordinary hairspray to dissolve dust and dirt.

Avoid displaying an arrangement where it will be frequently bumped against or knocked over to prevent shattering.

Opposite Page

The mauve and green color scheme in this topiary was achieved with eucalyptus, German statice, pepper grass, and pink ti tree.

The paper ribbon was attached to a floral pick, inserted into the styrofoam base, and then opened up at the bottom to form a bow.

Right: This small topiary was made from scrap pieces of pearly everlasting, roses, globe amaranth, German statice, nigella, celosia, larkspur, and pepper grass. The everlastings were attached with hot glue.

Below: A miniature topiary of dried rose buds was made by cutting each rose stem at a sharp angle and then inserting it into the small styrofoam base. The flower pot is decorated with sheet moss, German statice, and rose buds.

When topiary was a highly ornate gardening art in centuries past, the enthusiasm even found expression in elaborate and sometimes outrageous coiffures of aristocratic ladies.

Left: *Small pieces of roses, statice, caspia, and delphinium were hot-glued onto a base cut from styrofoam.*

Below: *Miniature topiaries from tinted sweet Annie are a beautiful way to use leftover pieces of everlastings.*

Whether this Valentine's topiary tree finds a home on your sweetheart's office desk, or makes a centerpiece for a romantic dinner for two, it radiates love with roses, larkspur, and moss.

Right: Initially designed as decoration for a wedding ceremony, this tall topiary (over five feet) is a lasting keepsake for the bride.

Stems of fresh boxwood were first arranged and picked onto a styrofoam ball and allowed to dry. Roses, statice, pepper grass, and magnolia foliage were then picked into the ball to form a colorful arrangement. Last, a long stem of ivy was picked into the ball and swirled down the tree's stem.

Left: *This Christmas topiary makes a festive centerpiece for the holiday season. The tree's stem is a large cinnamon stick that emits a light fragrance.*

The tree was made from pepper grass, red ti tree, artificial pine and berries, and seed pods from birch branches picked into a styrofoam base.

Several loops of red velvet ribbon were wired to a floral pick and inserted into the base to form the bow.

Below: *Stalks of wheat and oats were arranged and tied with cord to form these miniature trees. The stems were then trimmed to an even length and secured in decorative containers.*

The branches of a two-foot (61 cm) artificial Christmas tree were decorated with miniature red roses, statice, and red berries attached with hot glue.

Color Meaning Chart

Everlasting floral gifts with personalized meanings
can also be created with the historical meanings
of many colors.

Color	Meaning
Blue	Calm, rest, harmony
Brown	Comfortable, domestic
Cream	Intuitive mind
Green	Beauty, good fortune, youth
Orange	Supramental qualities, luck, prosperity, victory
Pink	Colors of the psychic region, love, honesty, allegiance
Purple	Power
Red	Physical strength, courage
White	Joy, satisfaction, purity, blessedness, peace
Yellow	Mental aspiration, discretion, discerning understanding

Right: A delicate porcelain-footed container makes a beautiful complement to this Victorian Christmas tree arrangement.

A tree-shaped styrofoam cone was first covered with a base of fresh ivy using greening pins. After the ivy dried, roses, heather, baby's breath, stock, statice, seed pods, and small white bows were arranged and then secured in place with floral picks.

Far right: German statice, pearly everlasting, and baby's breath were picked into a cone of styrofoam. The ribbon streamers were added with floral pins that are hidden under the ribbon's loops.

The spirit of this tree signifies purity, chasteness, joy, longevity, and peace at Christmas time. The white ribbon and flowers suffuse their meanings, while the red adds a touch of love and courage.

Below left: *Strawflowers, larkspur, globe amaranth, roses, celosia, and pearly everlasting decorate the branches of a small artificial tree. The flowers were attached with hot glue.*

Below right: *This small Victorian table-top tree was first decorated with a skirt of gathered red velvet ribbon hot-glued in place. Small bouquets of roses, globe amaranth, lavender, and baby's breath were then taped together and tucked into the branches. You can easily increase the fullness of the tree by tucking sprigs of baby's breath into bare spots.*

Right: *This holiday tree was made by hot-gluing a spiral of tightly-twisted Spanish moss up the tree's base and then gluing small stems of everlastings into the moss.*

The everlastings include roses, celosia, pearly everlasting, globe amaranth, larkspur, strawflowers, and pepper grass. A velvet ribbon hot-glued to the top of the tree and a skirt of gathered lace attached to the bottom add personal touches.

The base can be purchased pre-made at a craft supply store or made at home by wrapping grapevine around a wire stand.

Above: *A triangular-shaped piece of floral foam was decorated with a background of statice latifolia, clusters of celosia, goldenrod, and yarrow were then picked into the foam.*

Bouquets, Corsages and Tussie Mussies

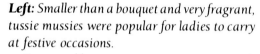

Left: Smaller than a bouquet and very fragrant, tussie mussies were popular for ladies to carry at festive occasions.

To assemble your own treasure, start with flowers with approximately the same length stems. Arrange the flowers in your hand and insert the stems through the center of the doilie. Secure the stems by wrapping floral tape around them, beginning beneath the doilie and continuing down the stems for a couple inches. Trim stems and cut floral tape. Finish with a ribbon bow to complement the flower colors.

Right: The blue, lavender and silver bouquet was arranged by height, beginning with the tall silver flowers held in the hand. Then blue and lavender were placed on top as the flowers were turned a quarter turn in the hand. This gives two layers which can then be loosely wrapped with wire. Shorter pieces of blue and silver were put together as little bouquets and tucked into the wire working around the larger bouquet so all sides are equal. A ribbon secures the stems and covers the wire and a protective tissue paper wrapper finishes the bouquet.

The robust red and yellow of this bouquet is a sunny sphere of joy, and acts like a tonic that can say, "Please get well soon.,"

Above: *This ball of dried rosebuds can be held as a bouquet for a wedding or used as a hanging decoration in the home. The rose stems were clipped short at a sharp angle, and inserted into a styrofoam ball. The lace ribbon was then wired to a short floral pick and inserted into the ball.*

Below: *A small bouquet of tinted star flowers was secured together with floral tape and pushed through a small hole in a doily. Small stems of baby eucalyptus were then hot-glued around the doily and a satin bow was hot-glued to the base of the doily.*

Opposite Page
Colorful strawflowers, statice sinuata, rudbeckia, and feverfew were wired together into a bouquet and wrapped with green floral tissue.

Below: Mixing traditional everlastings with wild flowers and grasses found on a roadside or in the woods can create beautiful bouquets.

Left: *These miniature bouquets rest in small doilies and are decorated with delicate ribbons. They can be used as Christmas tree ornaments, place settings, or decorations for a shelf of knickknacks.*

Below: *This bouquet of cockscomb, roses, nigella, achillea-the-pearl, larkspur, poppy pods, silver king artemisia, sweet Annie, and silver dollar eucalyptus combines both subtle and vibrant colors for a beautiful effect.*

Green growth and the splendor of blooming colors can be fashioned to adorn most any mode of dress, such as the corsage and lapel pins shown here.

Right: *Cockscomb, German statice, silver king artemisia, annual statice, wild yarrow, achillea-the-pearl, and simplicity roses were joined with soft lace and loops of colorful ribbon to form a special tussie mussie.*

Below: *German statice, pussy willows, roses, sweet Annie, statice, and caspia form a tussie mussie of varying texture and color.*

Opposite Page

Left: *Roses, baby's breath, ting ting, plumosa ferns, satin ribbon, and pearls were wired, taped, and arranged into a lovely wedding corsage.*

Below: *These small lapel pins were made by hot-gluing glycerin-preserved leaves to a small wooden base, and then adding tinted everlastings and ribbons.*

Above: These Victorian-styled tussie mussies make beautiful centerpieces for a formal tea, and smaller pieces of the everlastings were used to make matching napkin rings. The everlastings include roses, leptosporum, baby's breath, ivy, and boxwood.

Right: German statice, roses, bee balm, calendula, germanda, daisies, and statice form a large tussie mussie whose doily was creatively decorated.

A tussie mussie is easily converted into a unique Christmas tree topper by wiring in several long streamers of ribbon.

The bouquet of everlastings was made from simplicity roses, German statice, annual statice, silver king artemisia, wild white yarrow, pearly everlasting, achillea-the-pearl, and an assortment of wild dyed grasses.

Pressed Flowers

Pressing flowers is one of the simplest methods of preserving flowers, and the delicate, flattened petals and leaves offer unlimited design potential to create cherished gifts.

Depending on the type of flower and how much natural moisture it contained before it was picked, flowers will generally take from six to ten weeks to dry completely.

When placing flowers between the pages of books or blotting paper, be sure that none of the petals overlap or have folds or creases.

The greatest variety of designs can be achieved by separating flower petals, leaves, and stems before pressing, and then re-assembling them as you're arranging.

Left: This pressing board was made at home with several sheets of plywood and ordinary household tools. When using a pressing board, place the flower petals and leaves between two sheets of blotting paper to absorb moisture.

Some plants that press particularly well:

Wildflowers, such as Queen Anne's lace, clover, goldenrod, morning glory, and yarrow.

Herbs, such as salvia and mint.

Annuals, such as marigold, zinnia, everlastings, dianthus, and violet.

Greens, such as ferns, and the leaves and grasses of the flowers and shrubs mentioned above.

The only flowers and leaves that do not press well are those with a thickness of more than ¼″ (½ cm).

Pressing flowers and leaves between the pages of a heavy book is one of the oldest methods of preserving flowers. Collections of pressed flowers called "herbariums" that were collected by scientists and pressed in books over 400 years ago have been discovered and the flowers are still in good shape.

If you're pressing in large quantities and run out of thick books, you can use thinner books and weight them with bricks or other heavy objects.

Right: *Pressed flower paperweights can be made in just a few minutes from inexpensive materials. Start with a hollow glass mold (available in craft supply stores) and a small sheet of cardboard or mat board. Trace the outline of your mold onto the background board and cut it out.*

Arrange and attach your flowers and greenery on the cardboard, leaving a small border of space around the edges to apply a thin layer of rubber cement or other adhesive that will secure glass and paper together.

Each of these paperweights encapsulates a message: "May your dwelling be comfortable," says the housewarmer (top), and for graduation, "May you prosper with dignity, health, and good fortune" (bottom left).

Pictures and gift cards offer creative ways to make pressed flower gifts. The flowers and leaves are applied to mat board or gift cards with water-based glue that is applied with a small paint brush or the tip of your finger. If the glue begins forming unsightly clumps, simply add enough water to form a thinner consistency. Paste glues can be used to attach pressed flowers to cloth-covered diaries, photo albums, or scrapbooks.

Avoid working in damp, humid weather that may cause the flowers to re-absorb moisture and lose their natural shapes.

For the forest scene shown here, varying sizes of yarrow, artemisa annua, wormwood, and fennel leaves were used.

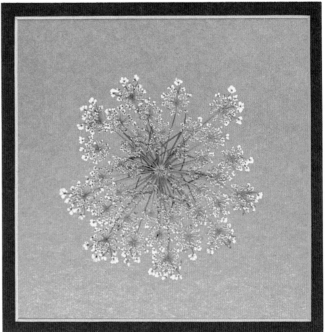

Above: *A single blossom of Queen Anne's lace can be matted and framed in a variety of ways. Queen Anne's lace presses best when it's picked about halfway through its blooming cycle, when it rests horizontally on the stem.* **Left:** *Pressed flowers transform ordinary note cards into cherished gifts.*

Opposite Page

Violets, coral bells, Queen Anne's lace, evening primrose, fennel, delphinium, hosta, obedient plant, and four varieties of salvia form this pressed flower picture.

Arrangements

Most arrangements begin by forming a specific outline or shape with a single material, and then filling out the arrangement with other flowers or greenery. Delicate materials are usually added last to prevent damage. (Note: A wide variety of instructional books on the formal elements of floral design is available in libraries and bookstores.)

Choosing an interesting container for an everlasting arrangement can be half the fun of creating a unique gift, so don't eliminate untraditional styles and shapes. Floral foam can be cut with a serrated knife to the exact size you need. Flowers with strong stems can be inserted directly into the foam base; while weaker-stemmed flowers will need to be wired and/or picked first.

Below: *Although these arrangements were created with identical everlastings (sumac, bayberry, artemisia, heather, horse tail, and viburnum), their looks are quite different.*

Below: *While these two arrangements were both made with goldenrod, statice, and sweet Annie, the addition of one unique everlasting adds a distinctive look to each. Stems of honesty were added to the vase on the left to add fullness and shape. Variegated bamboo leaves were added to the arrangement on the right to complement the design on the vase.*

Above: *Everlastings with sturdy stems can be inserted directly into a foam base custom-cut to fit a special vase or container. If the foam will show through the sides of your vase, moss or greenery can be hot-glued around the sides of the foam.*

These fan-shaped bouquets are rich with Victorian charm and contain herbal ingredients that will keep the home from harm.

Opposite Page

Hybrid mink protea, nerri folia, helani tulip ginger, rattle snake ginger, wheat calathea, banksia prionotus, fish tail palms, and Chinese fan palms were picked into a large styrofoam base to form this exotic arrangement of Caribbean flowers.

Below: These finger vases were prepared for arranging by cutting small pieces of very fine polyurethane foam and placing them into the fingers. The foam was allowed to slightly protrude over the top of each finger and was trimmed off with a paring knife after completing the arrangement.

The everlastings include: German statice, caspia, silver king artemisia, boxwood (wired before drying to allow for controlled shaping), lavender, larkspur, Dutch iris, and fern.

Left: Yarrow, black-eyed Susans, and sweet Annie were arranged in a milk can painted to complement the flowers. The black-eyed Susans were added to the arrangement last because they tend to be more fragile than the other flowers in the arrangement.

Opposite Page
Baskets make inexpensive and creative containers for everlasting arrangements.
Top: Miniature roses, caspia, and raspberry thistles fill a delicate basket.
Bottom: A small chunk of floral foam was wired to the basket, covered with Spanish moss, and filled with sweet Annie, miniature roses, pepper berries, and wood mushrooms. The swan was then hot-glued next to the everlasting bouquet, and small flower heads were hot-glued around the bottom of the basket.

Vine and wood baskets make natural complements to the subtle beauty of everlasting arrangements. Look for them in a variety of shapes and materials.

Below: *A bundle of birch branches formed the base for this centerpiece arrangement. Eucalyptus, German statice, ti tree, caspia, and pepper grass, and a large bow were arranged and secured with floral picks.*

Opposite Page
A rectangular piece of board from a felled Wisconsin barn was used as a base for this country arrangement. The everlastings were hot-glued to the board and include pussy willows, caspia, tree fungi, and tinted pepper grass.

Pussy willow, representing an unrealized promise of the future, is being shared here by two feathered friends. This would make a fitting gift for newlyweds.

Left: *Larkspur, roses, statice, gypsophilia, lavender, German statice, plumosa fern, and eucalyptus were used to create this basket arrangement.*

Below: *Small Christmas arrangements make beautiful, inexpensive gifts and can be placed in a variety of decorative containers. These arrangements were made with glycerin-presrved fraser fir, tinted sweet Annie, ti tree, formosa leaves, baby's breath, and artificial pine branches and berries.*

Left: *A tall, thin basket decorated with stiffened fabric was filled with an arrangement of scotch broom, eucalyptus, blue thistle, poppy pods, and lavender.*

Below: *Reminiscent of Old-World floral traditions, this basket was arranged with small bunches of lavender, ti tree, and edelweiss.*

Opposite Page

Top: *A simple fan shape of German statice and ti tree was arranged in floral foam cut to fit the pocket of a sea grass wall basket. Stems of dried roses were then tucked around the statice.*

Bottom: *Nigella, strawflowers, liatris, spiral grass, and a variety of silk flower stems were arranged in a large water pitcher.*

The fruit basket below is filled with flowers to decorate the hearth while out of winter use. Yellow is discerning and cream intuitive, while lambs ear adds mellowness with its silver of the moon.

Above: *This harvest horn of flowers was filled with sweet Annie, hydrangea, caspia, saraecenia lily, roses, statice, safflower, and tinted wheat stalks.*

Right: *A small chunk of styrofoam was wired to an antique bread board and covered with moss to form this unusual arrangement. A bouquet of honeysuckle and dried seed pods was then arranged in the foam, and additional pods and honeysuckle were hot-glued to the handle.*

The color pink—a favorite color of many designers—is also historically rich in meaning. Through the years it has been associated with the qualities of love, honesty, and allegiance.

Opposite Page

This large holiday wall arrangement used a long piece of felt-covered plywood as a base. The brass trumpets were attached first with hot glue, and then glycerin-preserved cedar and fraser fir branches were stapled to the wood to form the arrangement's outline. Smaller pieces of greenery, ti tree, roses, gypsophilia, and celosia were hot-glued in place, and a large bow was added.

Top right: Caspia, asparagus fern, dianthus, simplicity roses, Dutch iris (flowers and greenery were dried separately), German statice, annual statice, and wild grasses make up the soft colors in this small arrangement.

Bottom right: A small square of floral foam covered with moss was wired to the inside of a basket to form a base for an arrangement of pussy willows, pepper grass, and ti tree. The bird was hot-glued to the rim of the basket after the arrangement was completed.

Left: *Glycerin-preserved oak leaves, okra pods, nigella, money plant, bittersweet, salignum, and dried wheat stalks were arranged in a pumpkin planter for a holiday gift.*

Below: *A rectangular-shaped piece of floral foam covered with sheet moss formed the base for dried tree brackets, grass seed pods, bleached Queen Anne's lace, bleached hydrangea, and button flowers.*

Opposite Page
Larkspur, roses, statice, gypsophilia, lavender, German statice, plumosa fern, and eucalyptus were inserted into a chunk of floral foam cut to fit a glass bowl.

Small Gifts

Once you've made several everlasting gifts from the preceding chapters, you will undoubtedly have an enchanting collection of everlasting "scraps"—small pieces of leftover greenery or flower stems that were just too lovely to throw away.

The everlasting gifts in this chapter can be made with a minimum of time and materials. We hope you'll find them an inspiration for designing your own personal gifts.

Opposite page: *Christmas ornaments can also be made from a variety of decorative bases, such as crocheted stars, halved lotus pads, and circular shapes of paneling or cardboard. The everlastings were attached with hot glue and include rosebuds, annual statice, lavender, sage, heather, hemlock, pearly everlasting, and red berries.*

Above: *Beautiful hand-blown glass ornaments were adorned with dusty miller, celosia, roses, pepper grass, and ribbon attached with hot glue.*

Above: *Willow leaves and lavender were arranged and hot-glued to a light switch plate. Several coats of clear aerosol sealant were then added to prevent the everlastings from shattering during everyday use.*

Right: *Plumosa, statice, and roses were arranged and hot-glued to the face of an inexpensive clock. These particular everlastings were chosen because they can be pressed flat enough to allow the clock's hands to pass over them without causing damage.*

As a keepsake wedding box, give lavender blue for peace and harmony, white for joy and satisfaction, and fern for closeness and durability.

Even the smallest everlastings can transform an ordinary box into a keepsake gift.

Above: A wide ribbon was first shaped and hot-glued to the box. Small pieces of dyed star flowers and baby eucalyptus were then hot-glued into the bow.

Right: Several lengths of ivory satin ribbon were folded in half to create a pleated effect and then hot-glued to a hat box. Small bouquets of delphinium, baby's breath, and plumosa fern were then wired together and hot-glued to the ribbon.

Below: *Several small bouquets of delphinium, roses, statice, baby's breath, and palm were wired together with decorative pearls and tulle. The bouquets were then attached to the hat with corsage pins.*

Right: *Bay leaves, chive blossoms, rosebuds, statice, caspia, delphinium, and stems of pussy willow were hot-glued to the hat. A bow with trailing ribbons was attached last with hot glue.*

Opposite Page
Small wreaths make charming centerpieces when their centers are filled with decorative items such as candles or ceramic miniatures.
Above left: Roses, pepper berries, globe amaranth, sweet Annie, caspia, silver dollar eucalyptus, leiatrias, saraecenia lily, and wood mushrooms were hot-glued to a small vine base.
Above right: German statice, caspia, globe amaranth, statice, and strawflowers were hot-glued to a small moss base.
Below: Four small bouquets of roses, miniature carnations, baby's breath, and plumosa fern were wired and then tied to a satin ribbon. The ribbons were then tied onto a mirror, brush, and comb. The fourth bouquet was attached to the picture frame with hot glue.

Above: The removable base of a lamp was decorated with pitcher plants and small ferns. The everlastings were hot-glued into a small bunch of Spanish moss that was adhered to the base with adhesive floral clay.
Right: The rim of an inexpensive basket was first covered with tightly-twisted Spanish moss using hot glue. Small stems of celosia, roses, globe amaranth, larkspur, pearly everlasting, nigella, and pepper grass were then dabbed with hot glue and inserted into the moss at an angle. A length of ribbon was wrapped around the handle and a bow added to the front of the basket with hot glue.

Here is pink for love and honesty, carnation for helpful-ness and eagerness to please, rose for love, purple for power, and white for blessedness.

Inexpensive hair ornaments became cherished gifts when decorated with small everlastings.

Top right: *Globe amaranth, white statice, pepper berries, German statice, and a thin satin ribbon were hot-glued in place.*

Top left: *Caspia, hydrangea, and miniature roses were hot-glued to a hair comb.*

Below: *Inexpensive napkin rings were decorated with small pieces of everlastings and satin ribbon using hot glue.*

Right: *Small rosebuds were hot-glued to a styrofoam ball covered with sheet moss.*

Hanging over the punch bowl at a sweet sixteen birthday party are love, honesty, discretion, understanding, beauty, youth, and intuition—all in the guise of roses.

An Everlasting Garden

All of the plants in this garden can be dried and used to create beautiful everlasting gifts.

These everlastings add color to a winter garden.
- Bark
  - Franklinia tree, walnut, dogwood
- Berries
  - Pyracantha
- Blossoms
  - Bush Honeysuckle
  - Violet
  - Pansy
  - Crocus
- Evergreens
  - Boxwood
  - Ivy
  - Dwarf Conifers

Spring flowers make cherished everlastings.

Anemone	Pansy
Azalea	Privet
Crocus	Peony
Daffodil	Rhododendron
Dogwood	Rose
	Tulip

Summer flowers fill the garden with color and fragrance. Now is a time of abundance and inspiration.

Astilbe	Lamium
Brachycombo	Marigold
Day Lily	Poppy
Feverfew	Rose
Foxglove	Stock
Gladiolus	Strawflower
Hosta	Tiger Lily
	Zinnia

Autumn, with its lively gold and crimson colors, can be alive with fragrance too. These autumn everlastings are ready at traditional harvest time.

Comfrey	Poppy
Feverfew	Rose
Hosta	Sage
Monarda	Strawflower
Oregano	Thyme
	Zinnia

The garden layout shown here was designed to provide colorful, fragrant flowers and greenery throughout the year.

Perennials
1. Anemone
2. Astilbe
3. Comfrey
4. Compact Oregano
5. Crocus
6. Daffodil
7. Day Lily
8. Feverfew
9. Foxglove
10. Hosta
11. Ivy
12. Lamium
13. Monarda
14. Peony
15. Poppy
16. Sage
17. Stock
18. Thyme
19. Tiger Lily
20. Tulip
21. Violet

Annuals
22. Brachycombo
23. Gladiolus
24. Marigold
25. Pansy
26. Strawflower
27. Zinnia

Shrubs
28. Azalea
29. Boxwood
30. Bush Honeysuckle
31. Climbing Rose
32. Dwarf Conifer
33. Hydrangea
34. Privet
35. Pyracantha
36. Rhododendron
37. Shrub Rose
38. Rosa Rugosa

Trees
39. Dogwood
40. Walnut
41. Franklinia

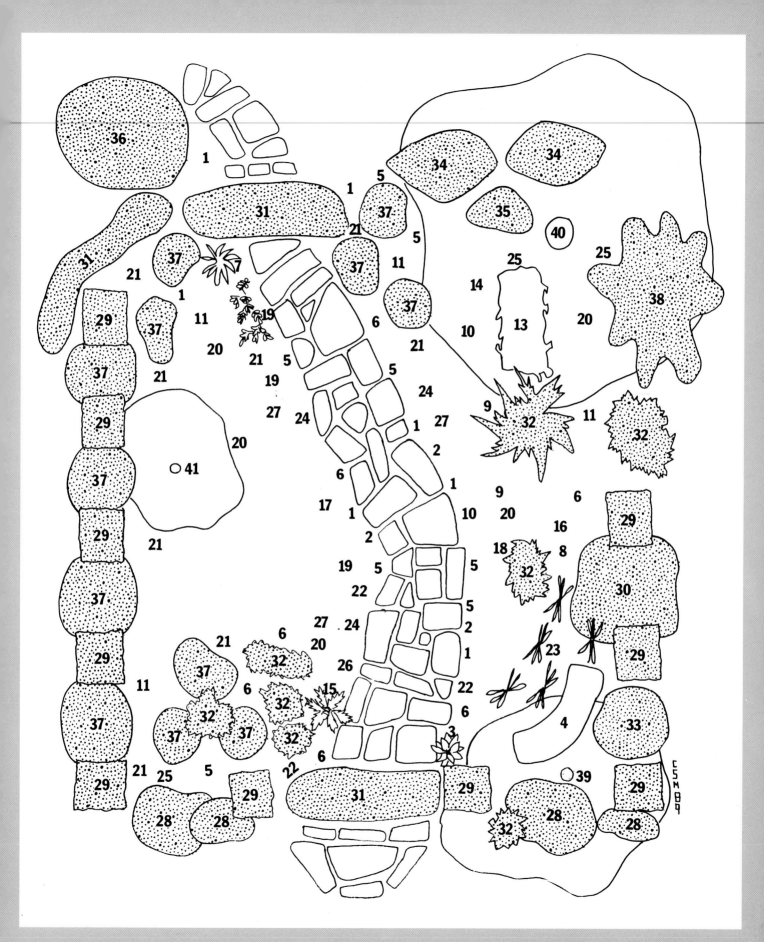

Contributing

Julianne Bronder studied at the American Floral Art School in Chicago. She now teaches floral design and does commissioned works. (Pages 42, 44, 54-top, 57-right, 82, 86-left, 116, 117, 119, 125-bottom)

Corinne Erb developed her flowing, natural style over 16 years of floral designing. She also incorporates her sensibilities as a painter, weaver, and multi-media artist into her designs. (Pages 52-bottom, 56, 57, 60-right, 84-left, 95-top, 133, 137)

Fred Tyson Gaylor, who has a degree in Creative Art from the University of North Carolina, taught art for ten years before changing careers to design showroom and movie sets. He enjoys using conventional materials in unconventional ways. (Pages 41, 46, 60-left, 86-right, 118, 120, 124, 127, 134-top)

Cynthia Gillooly is owner of The Golden Cricket, a floral design studio in Asheville, North Carolina. Her creative designs favor natural materials. (Pages 43, 113, 115, 122, 135-top, 136-top)

Linda and Debbie Greene are sisters and owners of Greene's Towne and Country Flower Shoppe in Hendersonville, North Carolina. Linda has a degree in Ornamental Horticulture and teaches floral design at a local community college. (Pages 39, 53, 85-right, 88, 98-top, 100-top, 114, 131, 132, 135-bottom, 136-bottom)

Jeannette Hafner grows most of the flowers she uses. She teaches drying and arranging techniques as well as design classes on making wreaths, topiaries, and decorated baskets. (Pages 40, 79-bottom right, 83-right, 90-top and bottom left, 129, 134-bottom)

Nancy McCauley gathers her own natural materials and uses traditional drying and dyeing techniques to create her innovative arrangements. From her studio in Oak

Designers

Ridge, Tennessee, she markets her items under the name of "From Gran's . . .". (Pages 38, 45-left, 58, 63-bottom right, 96-bottom, 97, 99, 101, 112, 125-top)

Sandy Mush Herb Nursery, Leicester, North Carolina, is the full-time passion of the Jayne family. They grow an extensive variety of culinary, decorative, and fragrant herbs which they sell, along with their wreaths, through their mail order catalogs. (Page 45-right, 51, 56-left, 59, 63-top, 89, 120-center)

Yellow Mountain Flower Farm is operated by Claudette Stewart and her two sons. She grows all the ingredients for her dried and pressed flower wreaths, which she sells at craft fairs. (Pages 9, 16, 17, 50, 52-top, 54-top right and bottom, 55, 62, 63-bottom left, 64-75, 91, 93-bottom, 94, 105, 106, 108, 109, 110, 111, 138, 139)

Also thanks to . . .

Carla Church (Page 130)

Darlene Conti (Pages 77-bottom, 79-top and bottom left, 92, 93-top, 100-bottom, 121-bottom, 126-top)

Ron Eggleston (Page 126-bottom)

Gail Martin (Pages 61, 80)

Anthea Masters (Pages 46, 87, 90-bottom right, 121-top, 128)

Michael Monroe (Page 123)

Deanne Nesbit (Pages 77-top, 78-top, 79-middle)

Tim Sigmon (Page 96-top)

Scott York (Pages 95-bottom, 128, 131-top)

Common and Latin Names

A

Anise hyssop . . . . *Agastache foeniculum*
Annual statice . . . . *Statice sinuata*
Azalea . . . . *Rhododendron*

B

Baby's breath . . . . *Gypsophila elegans*
Bee balm . . . . *Monarda*
Birch . . . . *Betula*
Bittersweet . . . . *Celastrus*
Blazing star . . . . *Liatris*
Bougainvillea . . . . *Bougainvillea*
Boxwood . . . . *Buxus*
Broom . . . . *Genistra*

C

Calendula . . . . *Calendula*
Carnation . . . . *Dranthus*
Caspia . . . . *Limonium bellidifolium*
Chinese fan palms . . . . . *Livistona chinensis*
Chive . . . . *Allium*
Cinnamon . . . . . . *Cinnamomum zeylanicum*
Clover . . . . *Trifolium*
Cockscomb . . . . *Celosia*
Coneflower . . . . *Rudbeckia*
Coral bells . . . . *Heuchera sanguinea*
Coreopsis . . . . *Coreopsis*

D

Daffodil . . . . *Narcissus*
Dusty miller . . . . *Artemisia stellerana*

E

Edelweiss . . . . *Leontopodium alpinum*
Elderberry . . . . *Sambucus*
Elsholtzia . . . . *Elsholtzia*
Eucalyptus . . . . *Eucalyptus*
Euonymus . . . . *Euonymus*
Evening primrose . . . . . *Oenothera biennis*

F

Fennel . . . . *Foeniculum vulgare*
Feverfew . . . . . *Chrysanthemum parthenium*
Fire thorn . . . . *Pyracantha*
Fish tail palms . . . . *Caryota*
Fraser fir . . . . *Abies fraseri*
Foxglove . . . . *Digitalis*
Fuchsia . . . . *Fuchsia*
Fuller's teasel . . . . *Dipsacus sativus*

G

Garlic . . . . *Allium sativum*
Geranium . . . . *Geranium*
German statice . . . . *Limonium*
Germander . . . . *Teucrium*
Globe amaranth . . . . *Gomphrena*
Globe thistle . . . . *Echinops*
Goldenrod . . . . *Solidago*

H

Heather . . . . *Calluna*
Holly . . . . *Ilex*
Honesty . . . . *Lunaria*
Honeysuckle . . . . . *Aquilegia canadensis*
Horehound . . . . *Marrubium*
Hybrid protea . . . . *Protea*
Hydrangea . . . . *Hydrangea*

I

Iris . . . . *Iris*
Ironweed . . . . *Vernonia*
Ivy . . . . *Hedera*

J

Jerusalem sage . . . . *Phlomis fruticosa*
Job's tear . . . . *Coix lacryma-Jobi*

L

Lady's mantle . . . . *Alchemilla*
Lamb's ear . . . . *Stachys byzantina*
Lantana . . . . *Lantana*
Larkspur . . . . *Delphinium*
Lavender . . . . *Lavandula*
Love-in-a-mist . . . . *Nigella*
Lupine . . . . *Lupinus*

M

Magnolia . . . . *Magnolia*
Maltese cross . . . . . . *Lychnis chalcedonica*
Marigold . . . . *Tagetes*
Mexican sunflower . . . . *Tithonia*
Mint . . . . *Mentha*
Money plant . . . . *Lunaria*
Monkeypod . . . . *Samanea saman*

O

Oat . . . . *Avena*
Obedient plant . . . . *Physostegia*
Oregano . . . . *Origanum pulchellum*

P

Palace purple . . . . *Heuchera*
Palmetto . . . . *Chamaerops humilis*
Pansy . . . . *Viola*
Passion flower . . . . *Passiflora*
Pearly everlasting . . . . *Anaphalis*
Pepper grass . . . . *Brassica*
Pine . . . . *Pinus*
Pinyon pine . . . . *Pinus edulis*
Privet . . . . *Ligustrum*
Pitcher plant . . . . . *Darlingtonia californica*
Poppy . . . . *Papaver*
Pussy willow . . . . *Salix caprea*

Q

Queen Anne's lace . . . . *Daucus carota*

R

Rabbit tobacco . . . . *Anaphalis*
Rhododendron . . . . *Rhododendron*
Rose hip . . . . *Rosa rugosa*
Rose . . . . *Rosa*
Rosemary . . . . *Rosmarihus*

S

Sage . . . . *Salvia officinalis*
Santolina . . . . *Santolina*
Sarracenia lily . . . . *Saraceniaceae*
Sassafras . . . . *Sassafras albidum*
Scotch broom . . . . . . *Cytisus scoparius*
Sedum . . . . *Sedum*
Silver dollar eucalyptus . . . *Eucalyptus cinera*
Spanish moss . . . . . *Tillandsia usneoides*
Starflowers . . . . *Smilacina stellata*
Statice . . . . *Limonium*
Stock . . . . *Matthiola*
Strawflower . . . . *Helichrysum*
Sumac . . . . *Rhus*
Sweet Annie . . . . *Artemisia annua*
Sweet Bay . . . . *Laurus nobilis*
Sweet woodruff . . . . . . *Galium odoratum*

T

Tansy . . . . *Tanacetum vulgare*
Tickseed . . . . *Coreopsis*
Ti tree . . . . *Cordyline terminalis*
Tobacco . . . . *Nicotiana*

V

Veronica . . . . *Veronica spicata*
Violet . . . . *Viola*

W

Wheat . . . . *Triticum*
Willow . . . . *Salix*
Winged everlasting . . . . *Ammobium*
Wisteria . . . . *Wisteria*
Wormwood . . . . *Artemisia*

Y

Yarrow . . . . *Achillea*

Photo Credits

Pages 2 and 3: From the gardens of Rasland Farms, Godwin, North Carolina. Photo: Rob Pulleyn.

Page 6: From the gardens of Nancy McCauley, Oak Ridge, Tennessee. Photo: Gary Albrecht.

Page 18: From the gardens of Nancy McCauley, Oak Ridge, Tennessee. Photo: Gary Albrecht.

Page 20, left: From the gardens of Nancy McCauley, Oak Ridge, Tennessee. Photo: Gary Albrecht.

Page 21: From the gardens of Nancy McCauley, Oak Ridge, Tennessee. Photo: Gary Albrecht.

Index

Bibliography

Cunningham, Scott
     The Magic of Herbs. St. Paul, Minnesota: Uewellyn Publications, 1986.

Erichsen-Brown, Charlotte
     Medicinal and Other Uses of North American Plants. New York: Dover Publications, 1974.

Gerard, John
     John Gerard the Herbal. New York: Dover Publications, 1975. Originally printed in 1633.

Meyer, Clarence
     Fifty Years of the Herbalist Almanac. Glenwood, Illinois: Meyer Books, 1977.

Pulleyn, Rob
     The Wreath Book. New York: Sterling/ Lark, 1988.

Rose, Jeanne
     Jeanne Rose's Herbal Body Book. San Francisco, California: Jeanne Rose, 1988.

Shaudys, Phyllis
     The Pleasure of Herbs. Pownal, Vermont: Storey Communications, 1986.

Wilder, Louise B.
     The Fragrant Garden. New York: Dover Publications, 1974.

Flowers and Their Messages. India, 1973. Translated from the French *Le Role des Fleurs,* 1953.

The Language of Flowers. London: Michael Joseph, Ltd., 1968.

New English Dictionary on Historical Principles. Oxford, England: Clarendon Press, 1901.

Rodale's Illustrated Encyclopedia of Herbs. Emmaus, Pennsylvania: Rodale Press, 1987.